AF413589

Phocabulary

Photography And Words

Chris Van Kirk

An • chor

/ ang ker /

noun

a heavy object attached to a rope or chain and used to moor a vessel to the sea bottom, typically one having a metal shank with a ring at tone end for the rope and a pair of curved and/or barbed flukes at the other.

verb (with object)

1. to moor (a ship) to the sea bottom

2. Act as an in studio newscaster for a tele vision program or sporting event

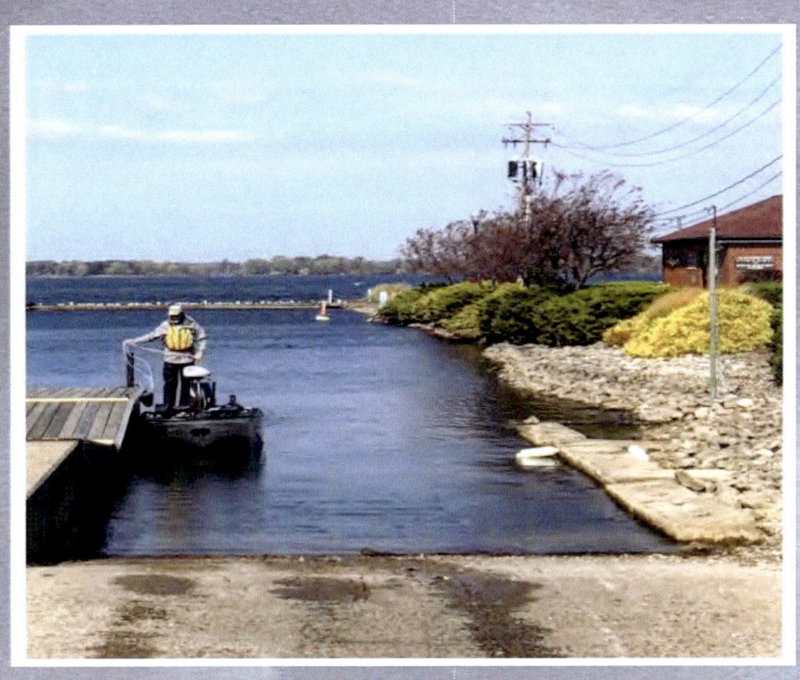

"Like an Anchor"

Tossed about in the sea of life,
As sailors we become navigator:
Hoping fate's dark storm will soon pass by
And it's swells rescind their anger.

Like Haley's comet from light years away
That has traveled through spaces none darker,
We've no guidance but very space-time itself
An Icy tail her luminous marker.

Maybe she tries to draw in the sky
A sign for those willing to read,
As of which way to turn when uncertainty rings,
So that call we on longer need heed.

So if a rock can inspire for millions to gaze
Then these words, let both your eyes hear,
Hold tight, like an anchor, to those whom you cherish,
While still loving the one in the mirror.

-CVK

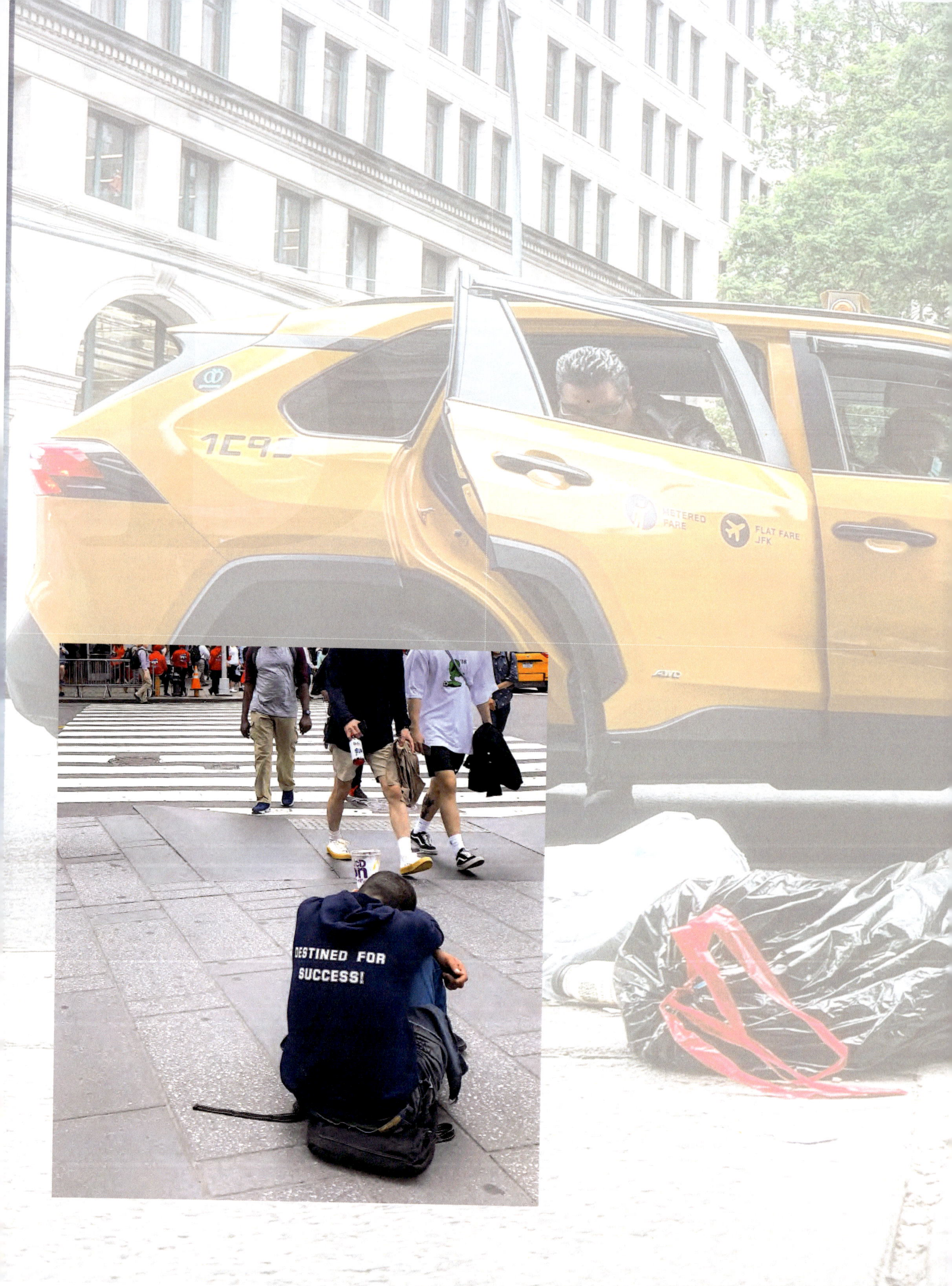

METERED FARE
FLAT FARE JFK
AWD
DESTINED FOR SUCCESS!

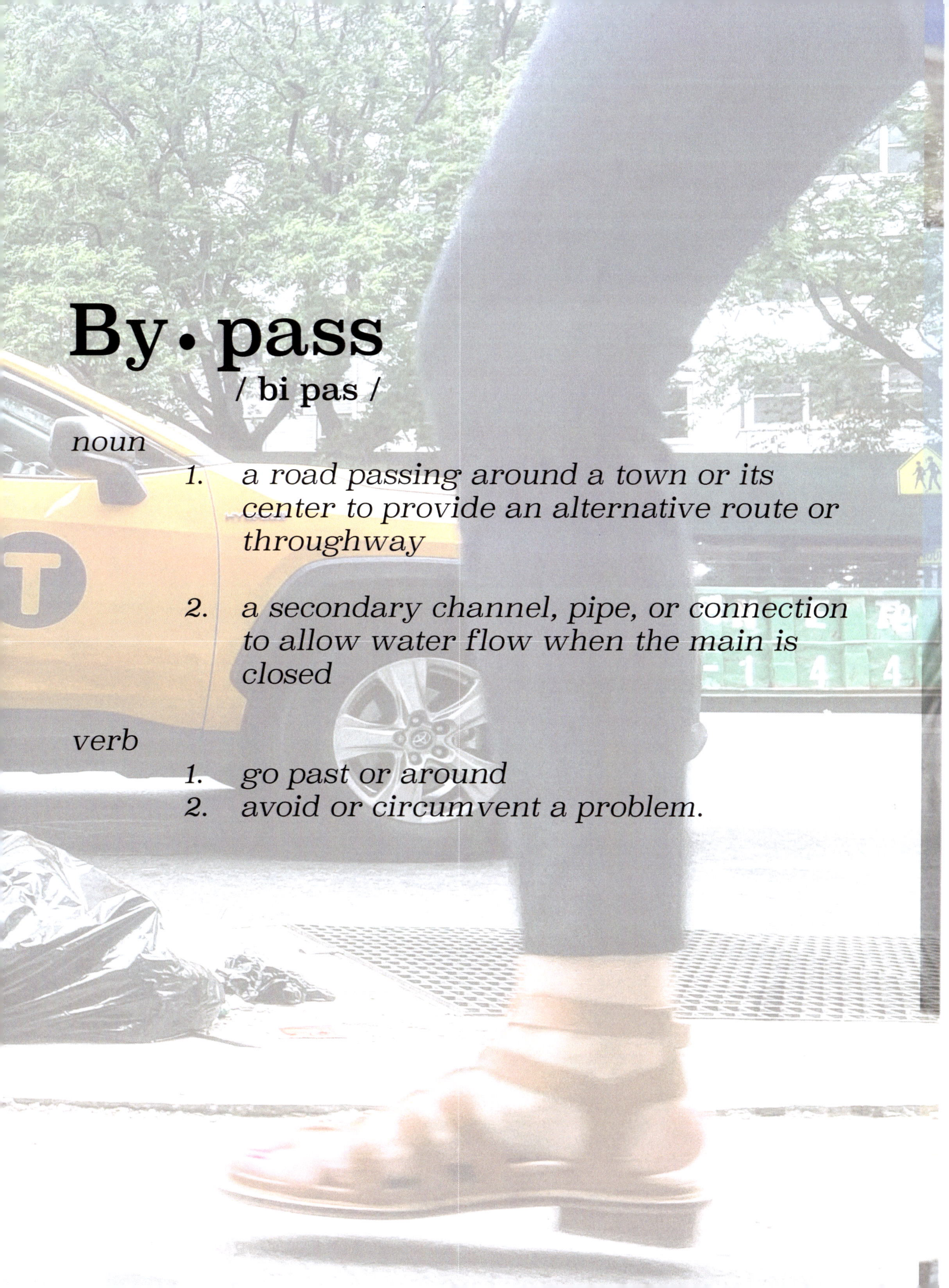

By·pass

/ bi pas /

noun

1. a road passing around a town or its center to provide an alternative route or throughway

2. a secondary channel, pipe, or connection to allow water flow when the main is closed

verb

1. go past or around
2. avoid or circumvent a problem.

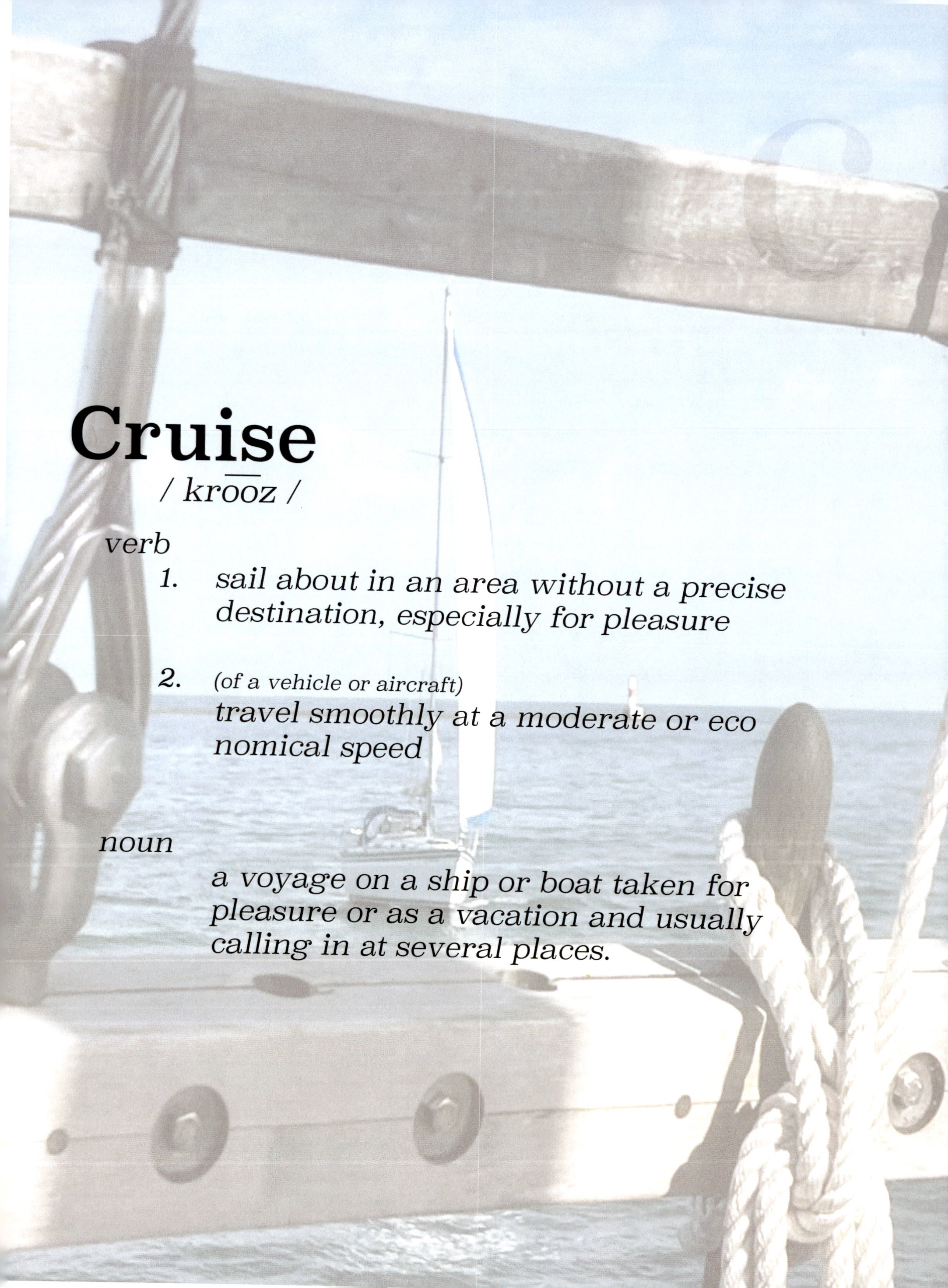

Cruise

/ kro͞oz /

verb

1. sail about in an area without a precise destination, especially for pleasure

2. (of a vehicle or aircraft) travel smoothly at a moderate or economical speed

noun

a voyage on a ship or boat taken for pleasure or as a vacation and usually calling in at several places.

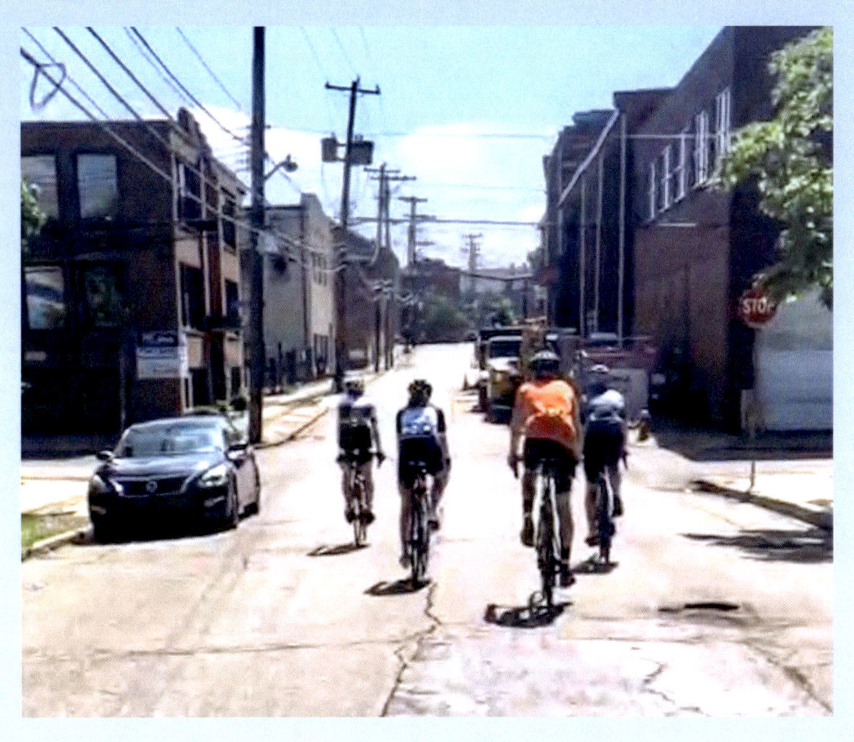

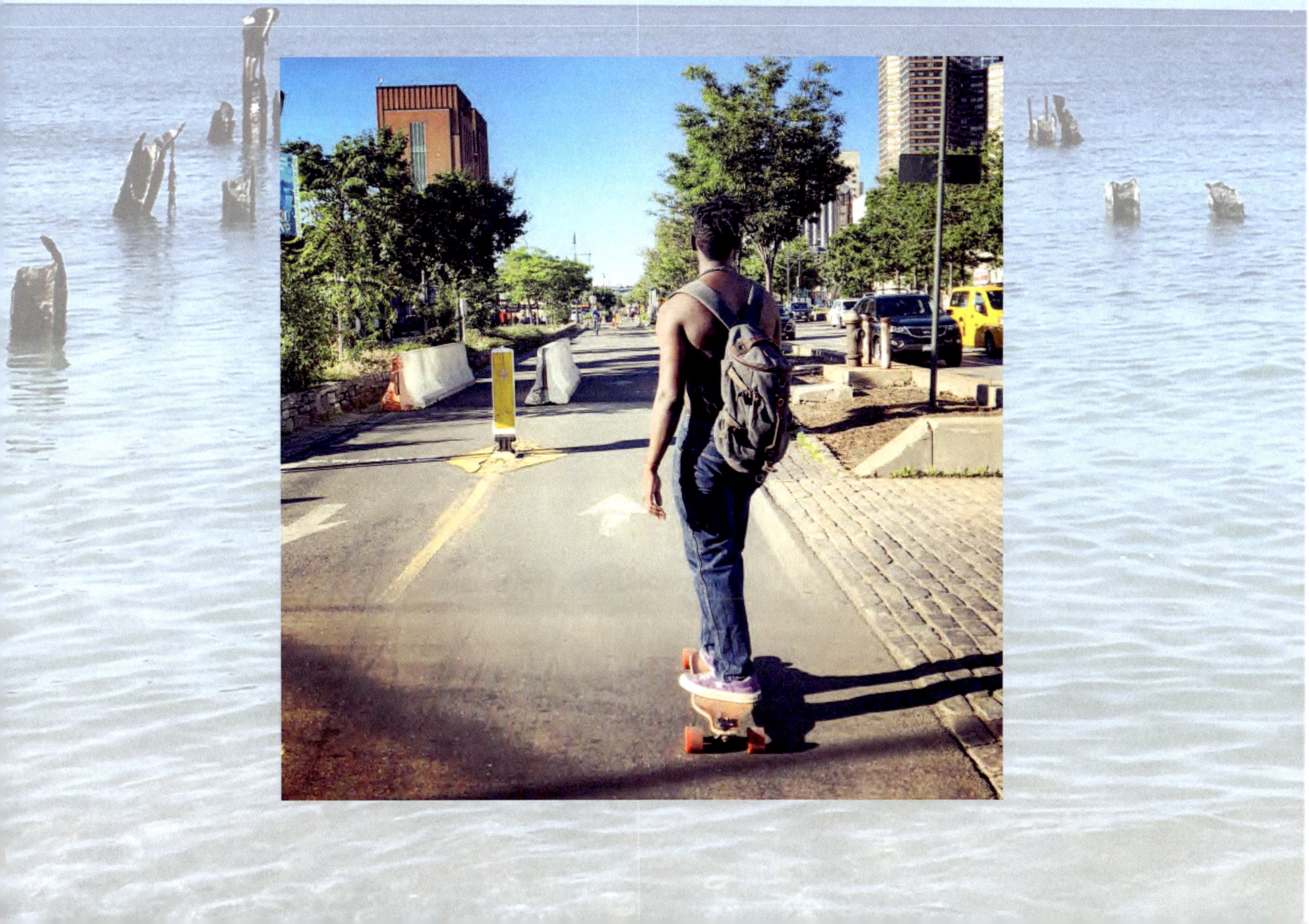

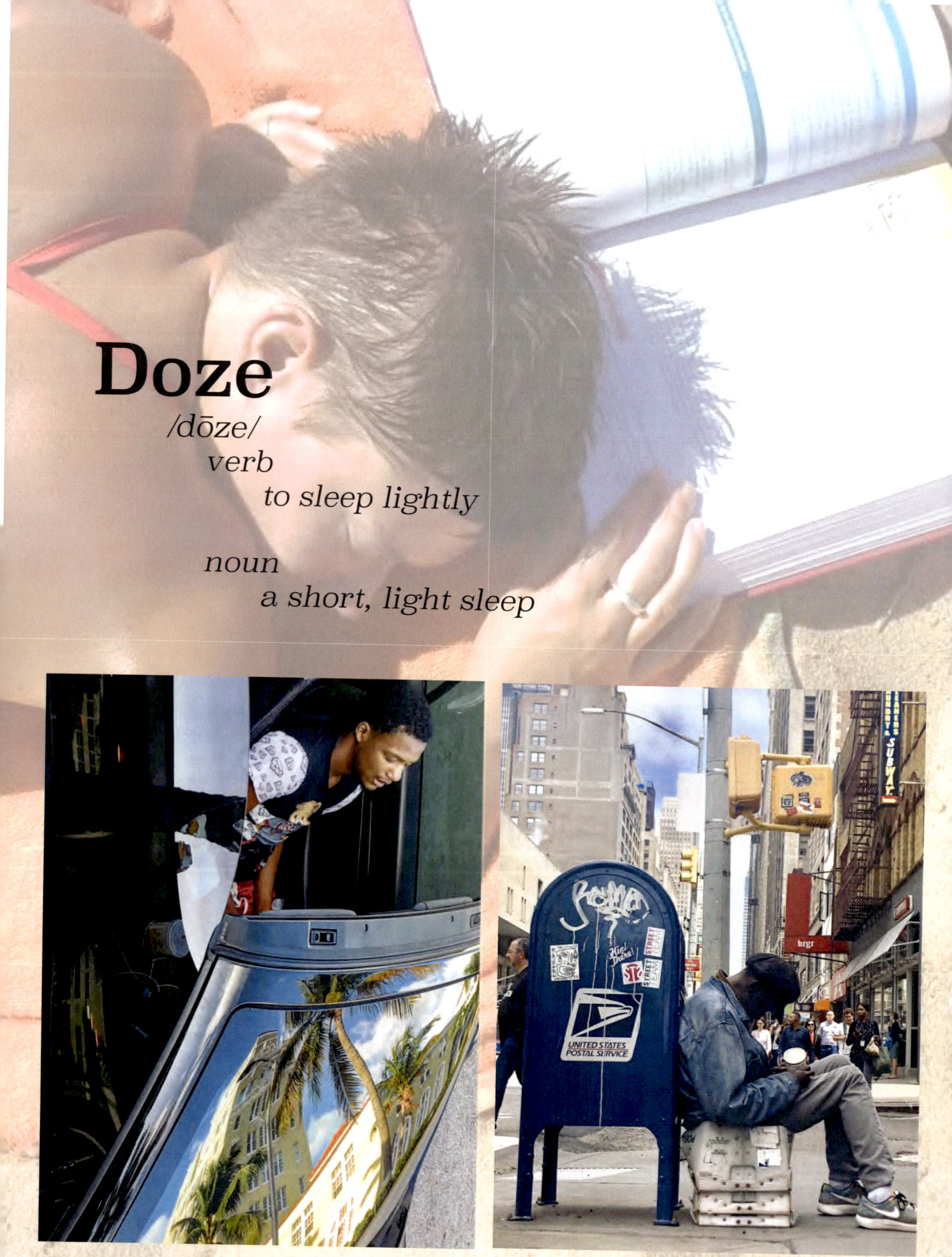

Doze
/dōze/
verb
to sleep lightly

noun
a short, light sleep

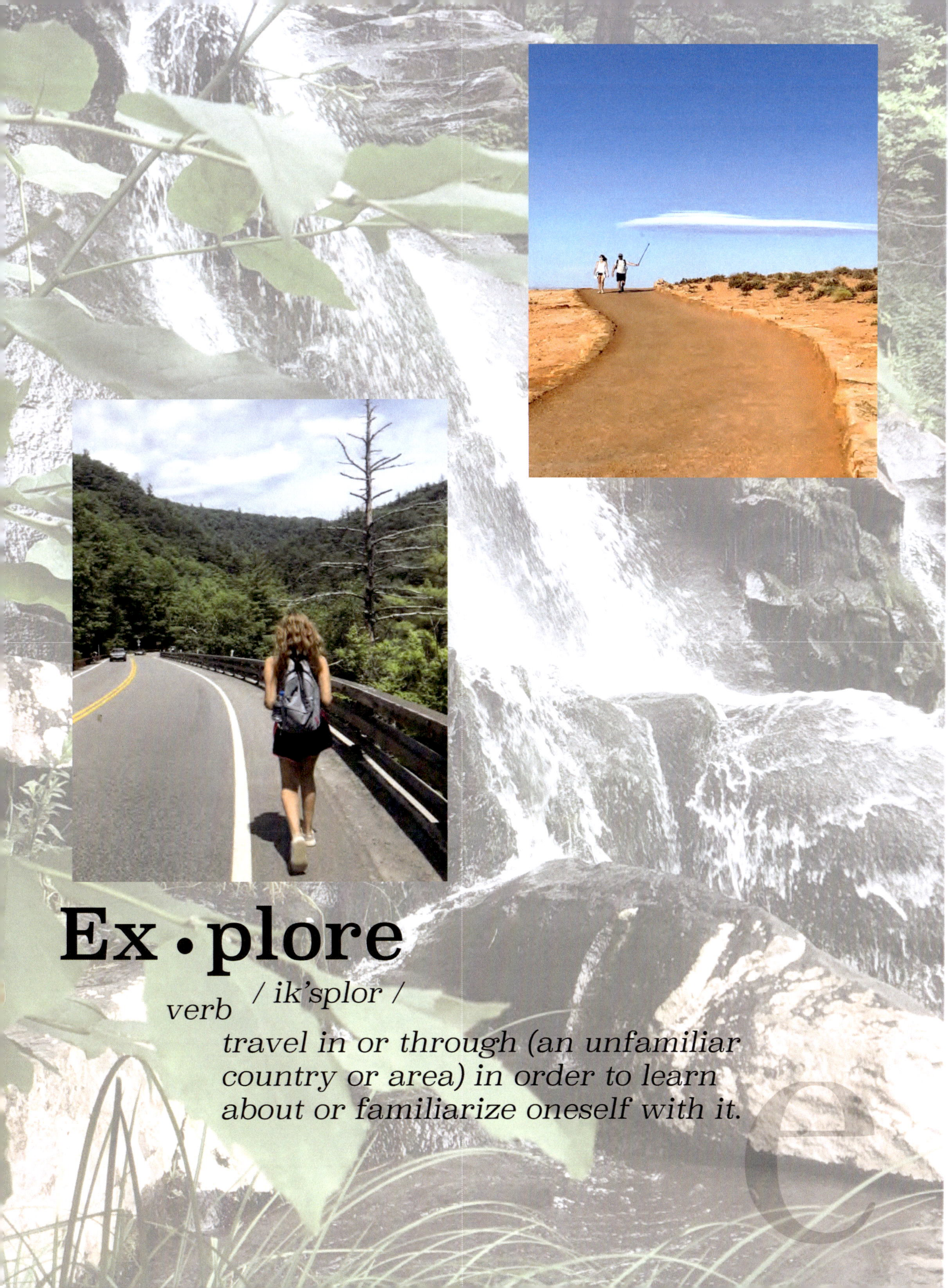

Ex•plore
/ ik'splor /
verb
travel in or through (an unfamiliar
country or area) in order to learn
about or familiarize oneself with it.

Find

/fīnd/

verb

1. discover or perceive by chance or unexpectedly
2. recognize or discover (something) to be present:

noun

1. a discovery of something valuable, typically something of archaeological interest;

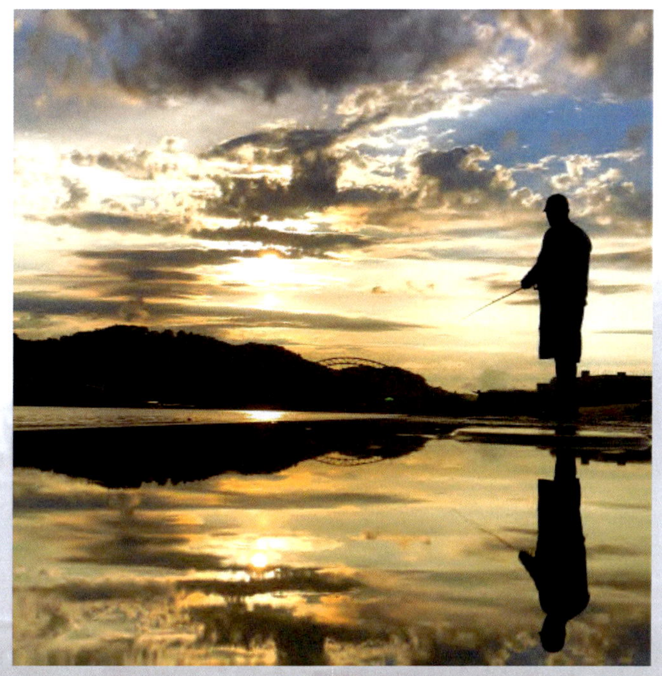

"Find"

The childhood game of hide and seek,
a preemptive metaphore
of all the wrong places I'd search in life
to see Purpose hide his face more.

But when I turned to a higher ground,
Self-loathing's sea I escaped
A guide-free lad fled their guilt-free lies,
To the land where the real me was shaped.

With little more than a dream for my future
And my gut saying, "take the leap,"
I left the place where I had no place,
A non-believer, so stamped a creep.

And to this day my eyes remain open,
That to new light I could n'er be blind;
So a life of love and happiness,
I am sure to finally find.

-CVK

Grow

/ grō /

verb

1. (of a living thing) undergo natual development by increasing in size and changing physically; progress to maturity.

2. become larger or greater over a period of time; increase.

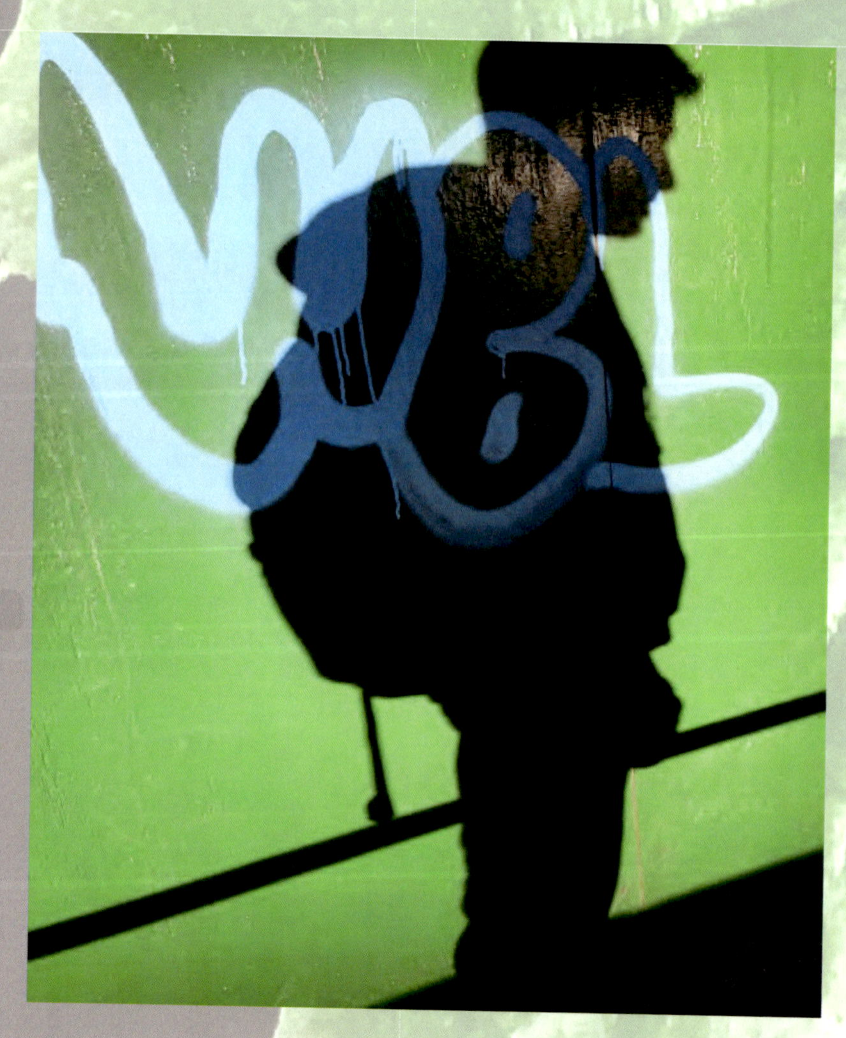

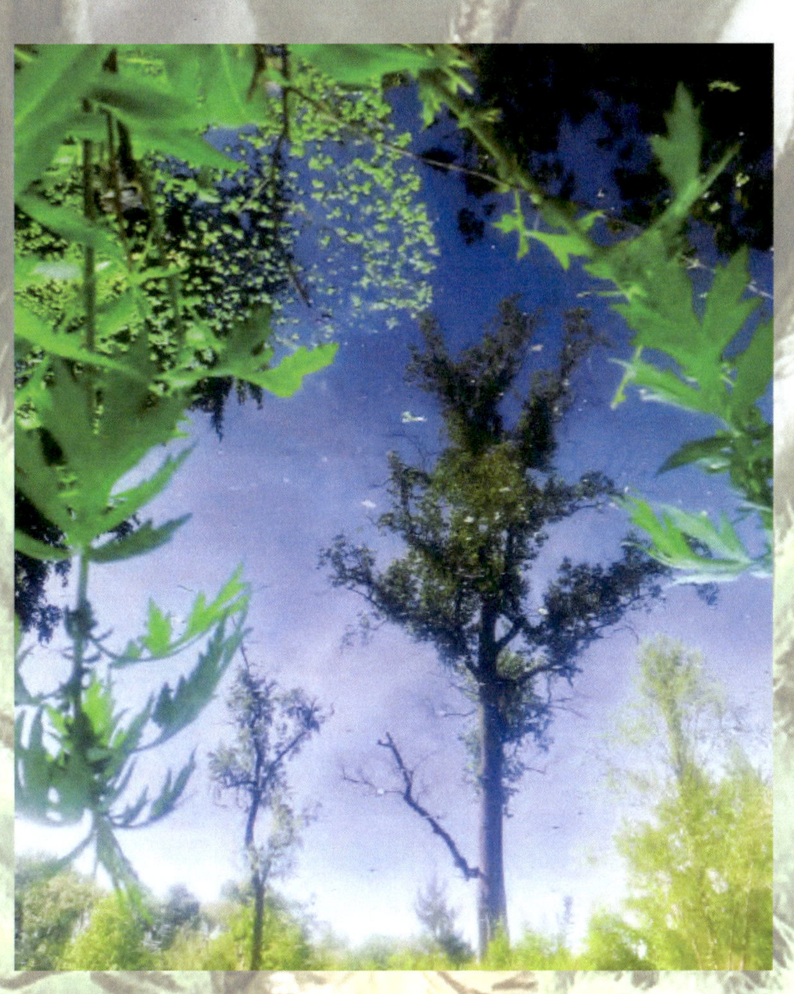

"Grow"

The ebb and flow, of all we know,
and the knowledge we have yet to obtain,
Should push us to learn and to better ourselves;
Strive to comprehend what we can't yet explain.

The size of the universe and it's trillions of stars,
Should cause humans, on this, to agree;
The amount we don't know exceeds what we do,
So to you this I now humbly plea.

Love thy neighbor, not just those next door,
For our race is human we know,
And never stop looking to learn something new,
So like seeds, we continually grow.

-CVK

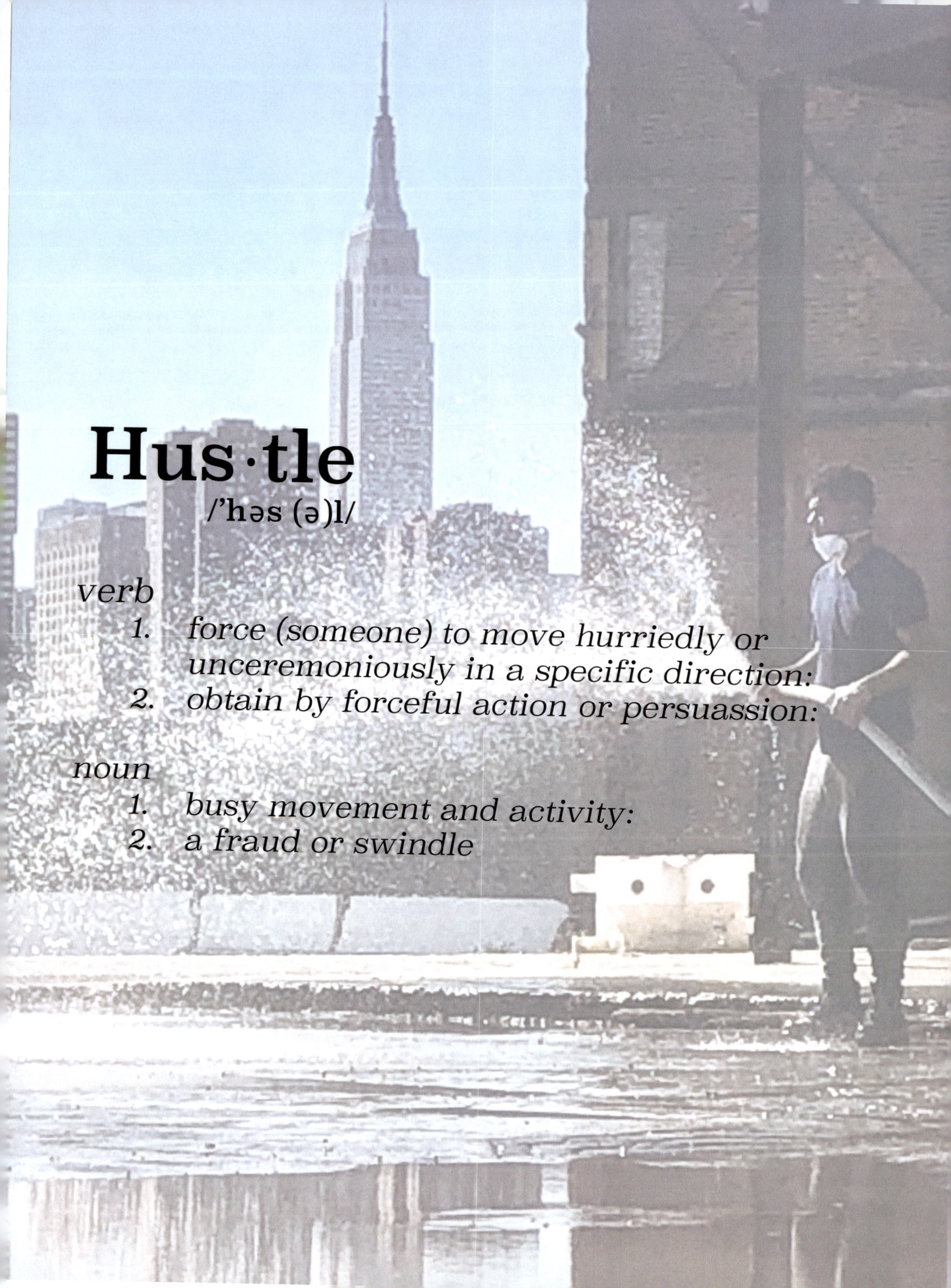

Hus·tle
/ˈhəs (ə)l/

verb
1. force (someone) to move hurriedly or unceremoniously in a specific direction:
2. obtain by forceful action or persuassion:

noun
1. busy movement and activity:
2. a fraud or swindle

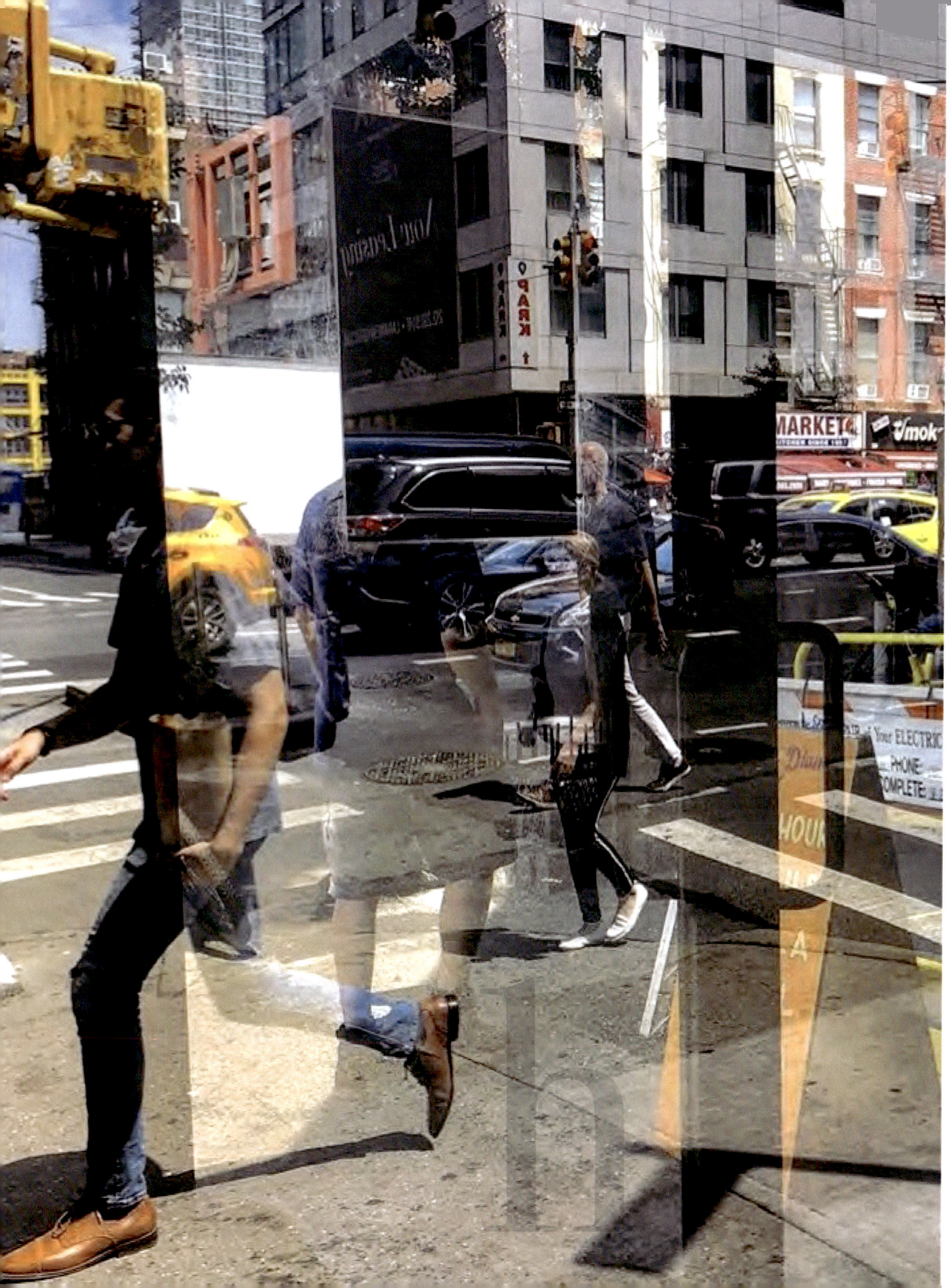

Il·lu·mi·nate

/i'loomə,nat/

verb

1. make (something) visible or bright by shining light on it; light it up

2. help to clarify or explain

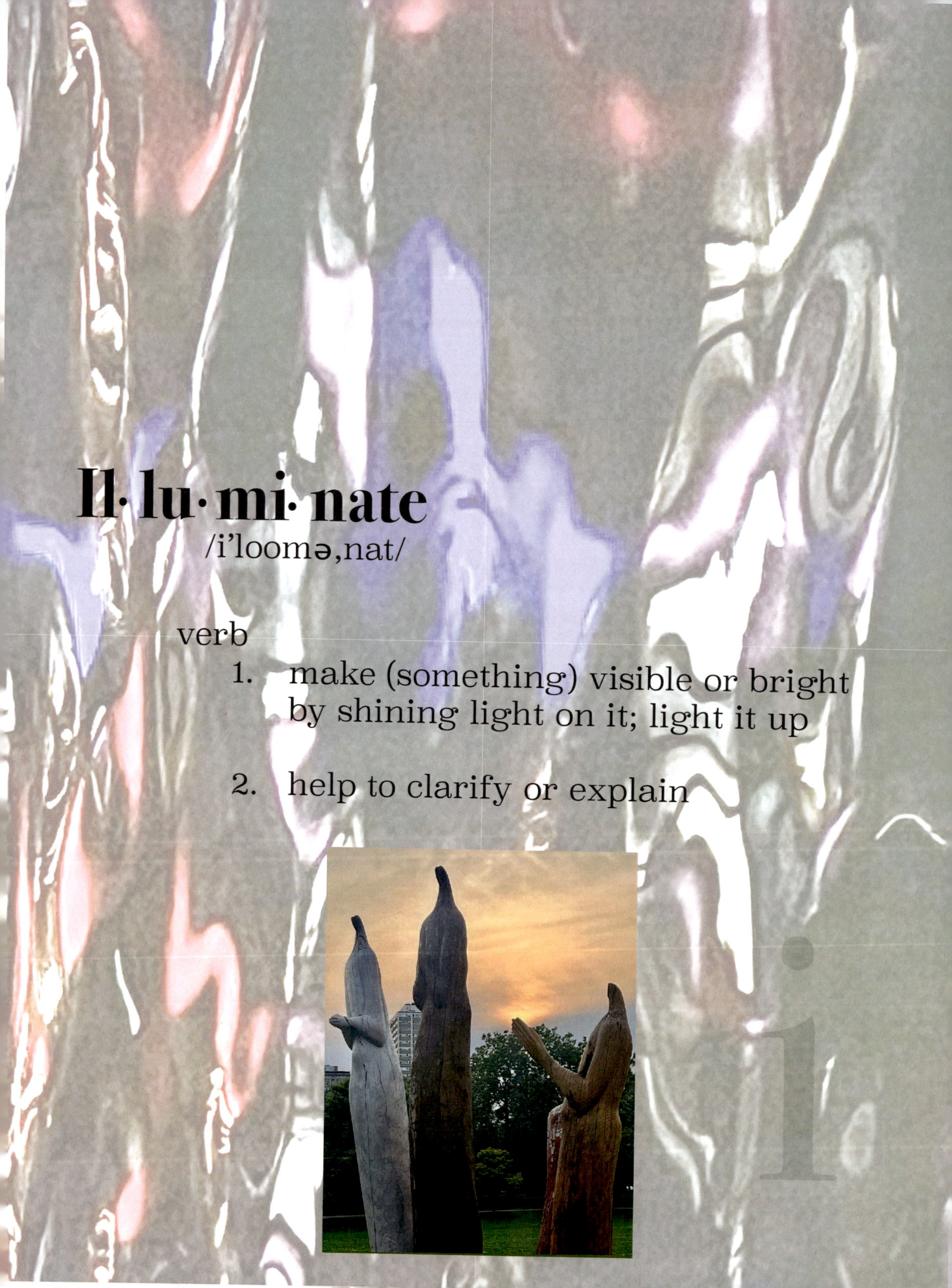

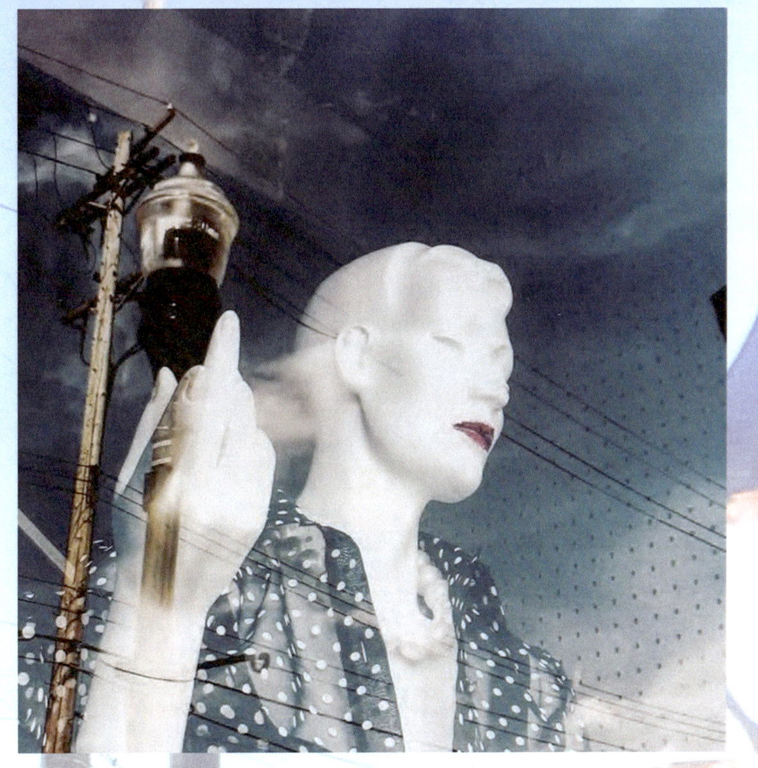

"ILLUMINATE"

We ruminate and concentrate on things we desire,
Implement thought, put work in; perspire.
So dreams only seen in the darkness of night
Like David, from marble, can be brought to light.

When along the way struggle tries to extinguish,
The light you shine, just know in plain English
Thats the very thing that will give you your power,
the struggle, the fight, the refusal to cower

To the slings and arrows life hesitates not to throw,
But if we persevere, our success we'll know
For stars shine their brightest, the darker the night
Maybe they shine to show us they won their fight.

So Hold your light high, for the world is lost,
Hold tight to your loved ones at any cost.
Negative energy eliminate
So your shine, their darkness, will illuminate.

-CVK

Jump
/jəmp/

verb

1. push oneself and into the air by using the muscles in one's legs and feet:

2. (of a person) move suddenly and quickly in a specified.

noun

1. an act of jumping from a surface by pushing upward with one's legs and feet:

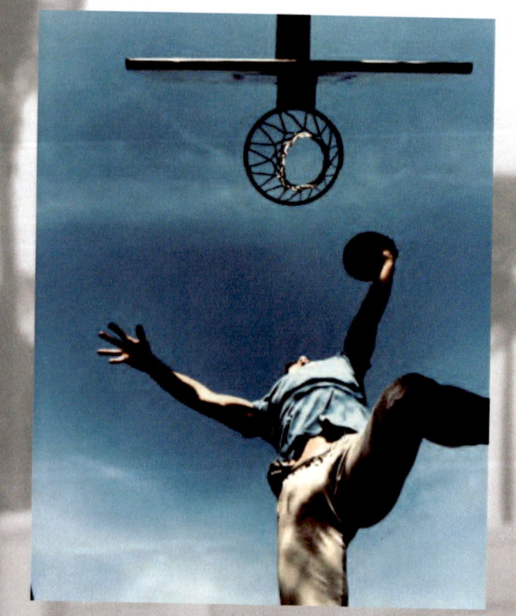

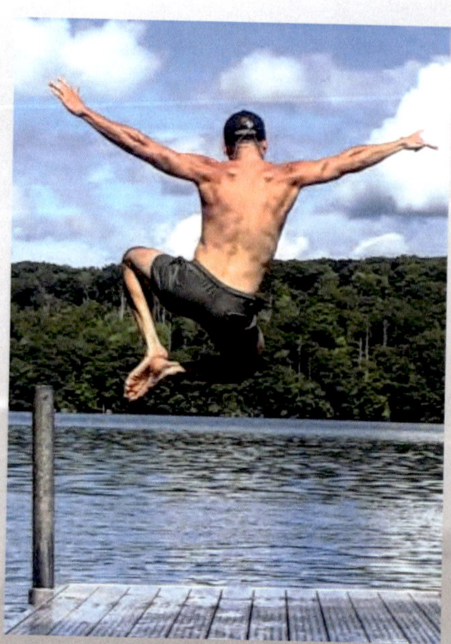

Know

/nō/

verb
1. be aware of through observation, inquiry, or information

2. have developed a relationship with (someone) through meeting and spending time with them; be familiar or friendly with:

Blind misconception; cultish direction
obsessed with a book; and their Lord's resurrection.
So all-in they went, living Bible hell-bent,
other thoughts and ideas, considered dissent.

The forbidden idea to question the Word,
Was something I saw as bizarre and absurd,
So I questioned everything, in search of the truth
Making me their black sheep, stamped 'Prodigal Youth'

Yet their fatted calf has grown to a cow
Because hateful religion, I will not allow
To be my story, so I picked up a pen
To write my own future, new adventures begin

So forward I'll move, with shed chains of sadness
Precious time no longer being lost to their madness.

-CVK

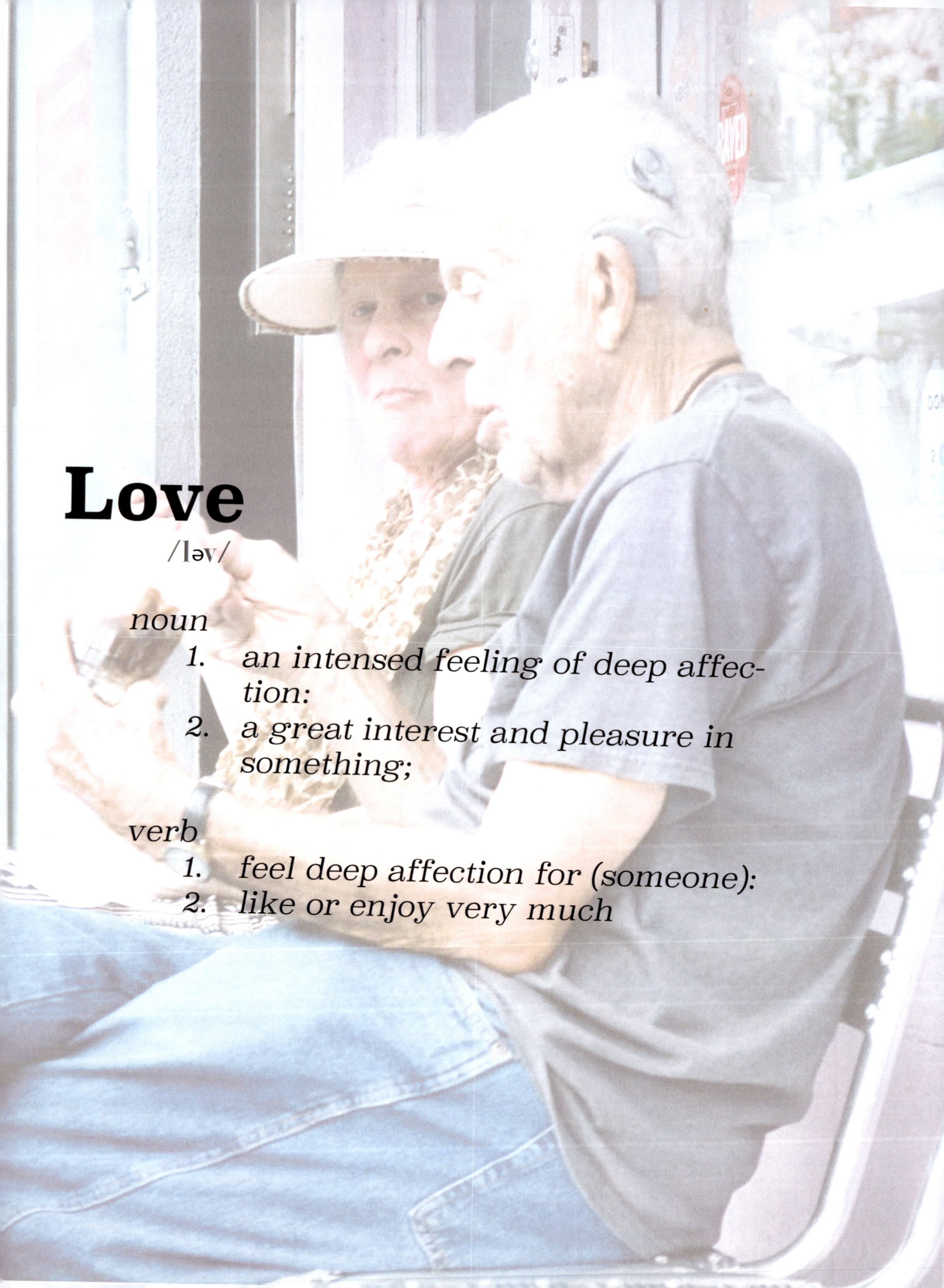

Love

/ləv/

noun

1. an intensed feeling of deep affection:
2. a great interest and pleasure in
   something;

verb

1. feel deep affection for (someone):
2. like or enjoy very much

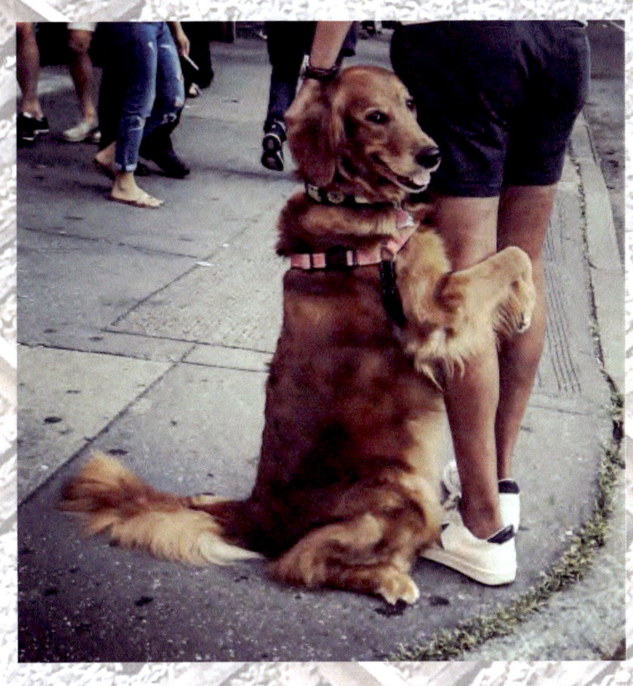

"LOVE'S GAME"

The tears I cry for you , my sweet,
are salty like the sea.
they burn my eyes, but yet comprise
a drop of love for thee.
I learn the pain from missing you,
heals only by crawling time,
I cried, I longed, I mourned with song
and now cope with written rhyme.
Remember the good times; I'll do the same .
while vowing never again
to be fooled by Love's Game.

-CVK

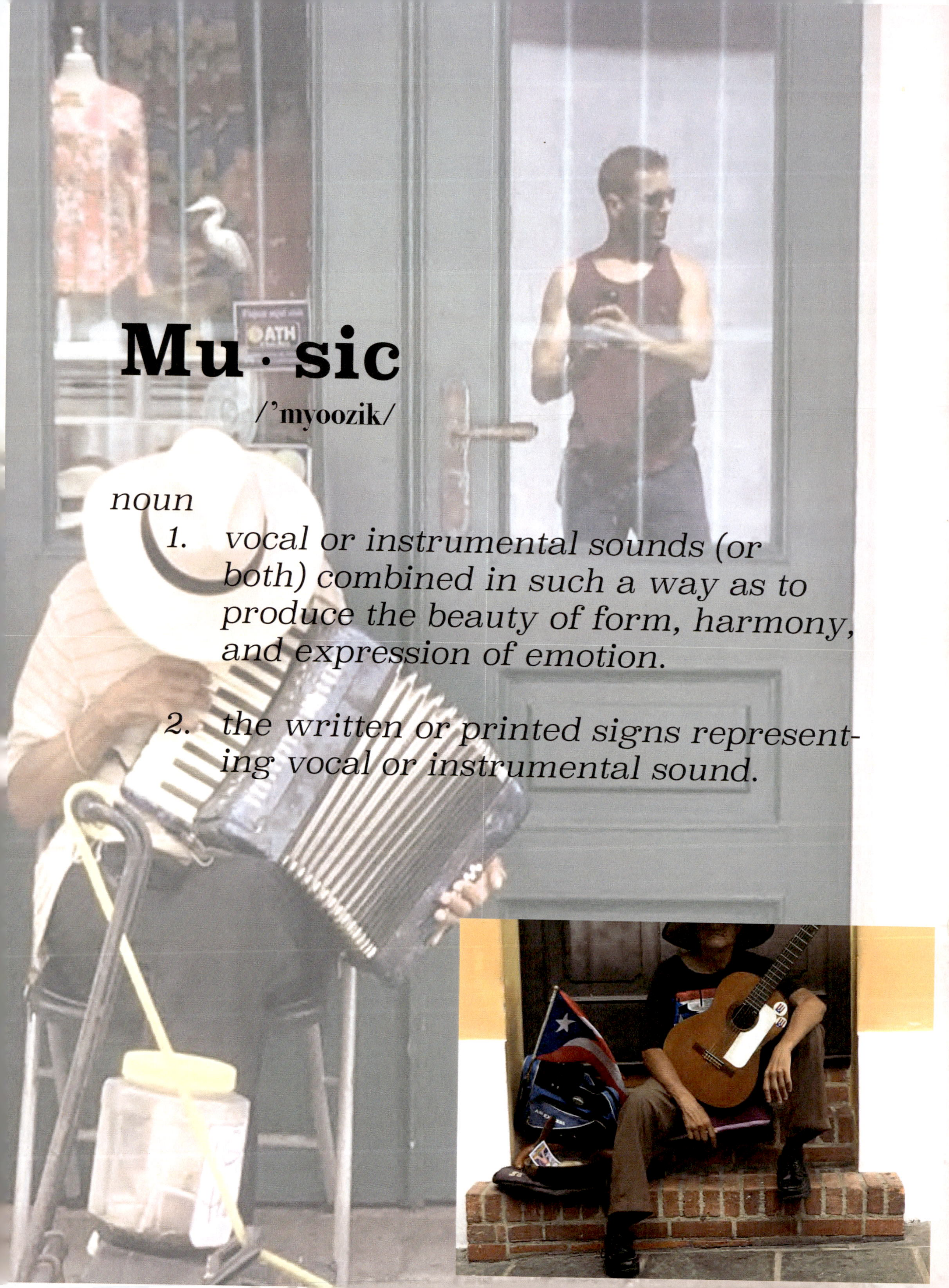

Mu · sic

/'myoozik/

noun

1. vocal or instrumental sounds (or both) combined in such a way as to produce the beauty of form, harmony, and expression of emotion.

2. the written or printed signs representing vocal or instrumental sound.

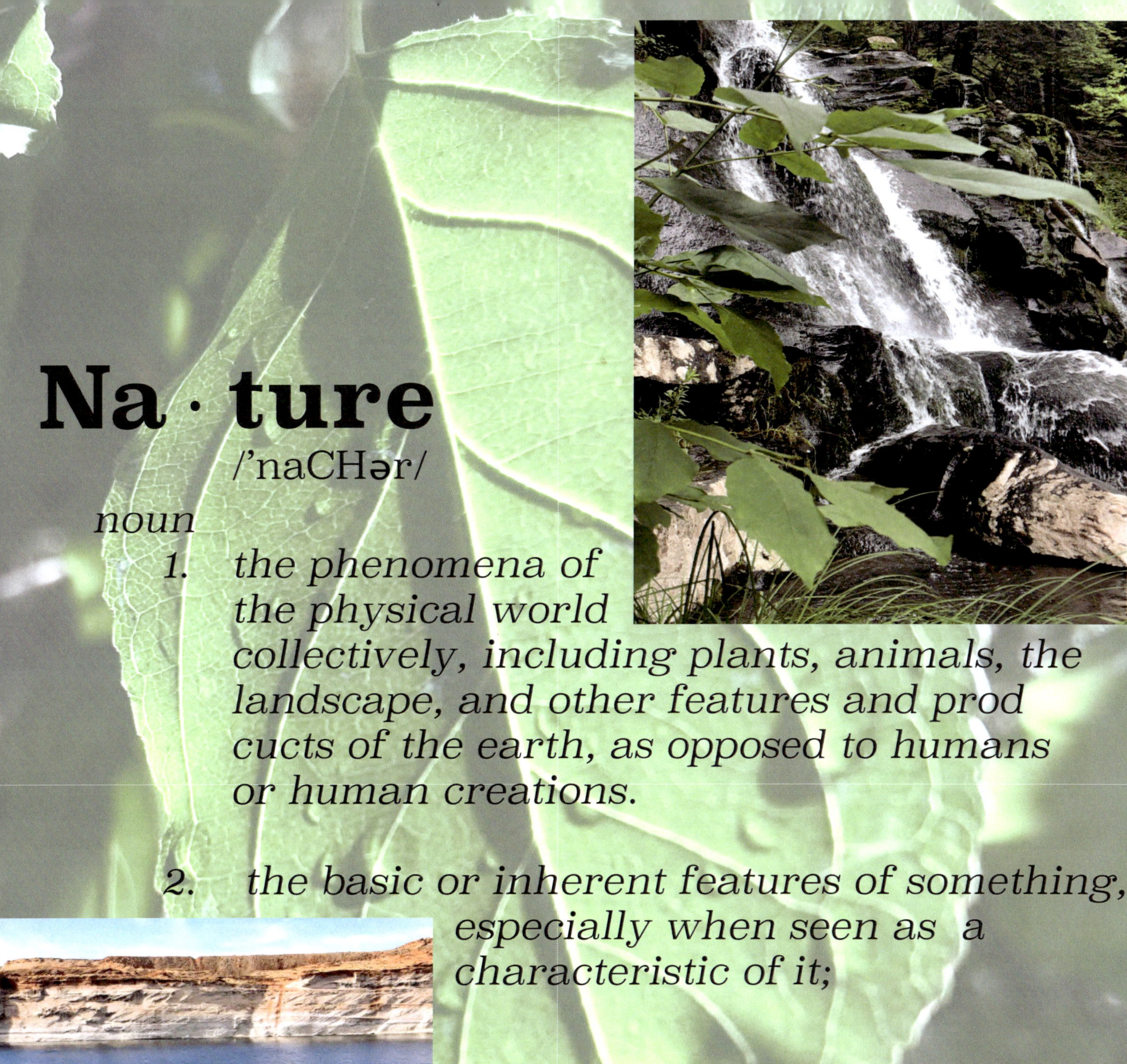

Na · ture

/ˈnaCHər/

noun

1. the phenomena of the physical world collectively, including plants, animals, the landscape, and other features and prod cucts of the earth, as opposed to humans or human creations.

2. the basic or inherent features of something, especially when seen as a characteristic of it;

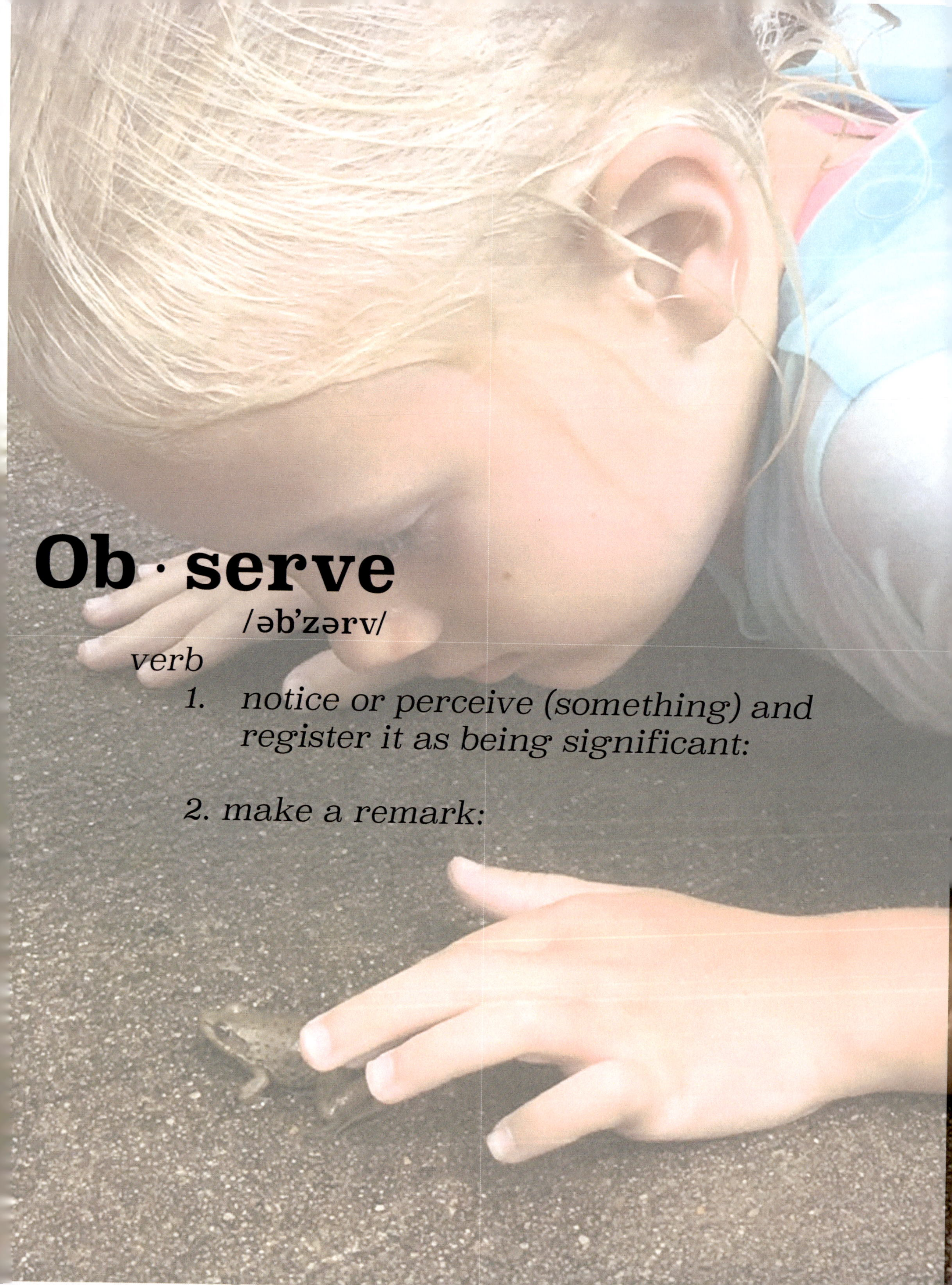

Ob · serve
/əb'zərv/
verb
1. notice or perceive (something) and register it as being significant:
2. make a remark:

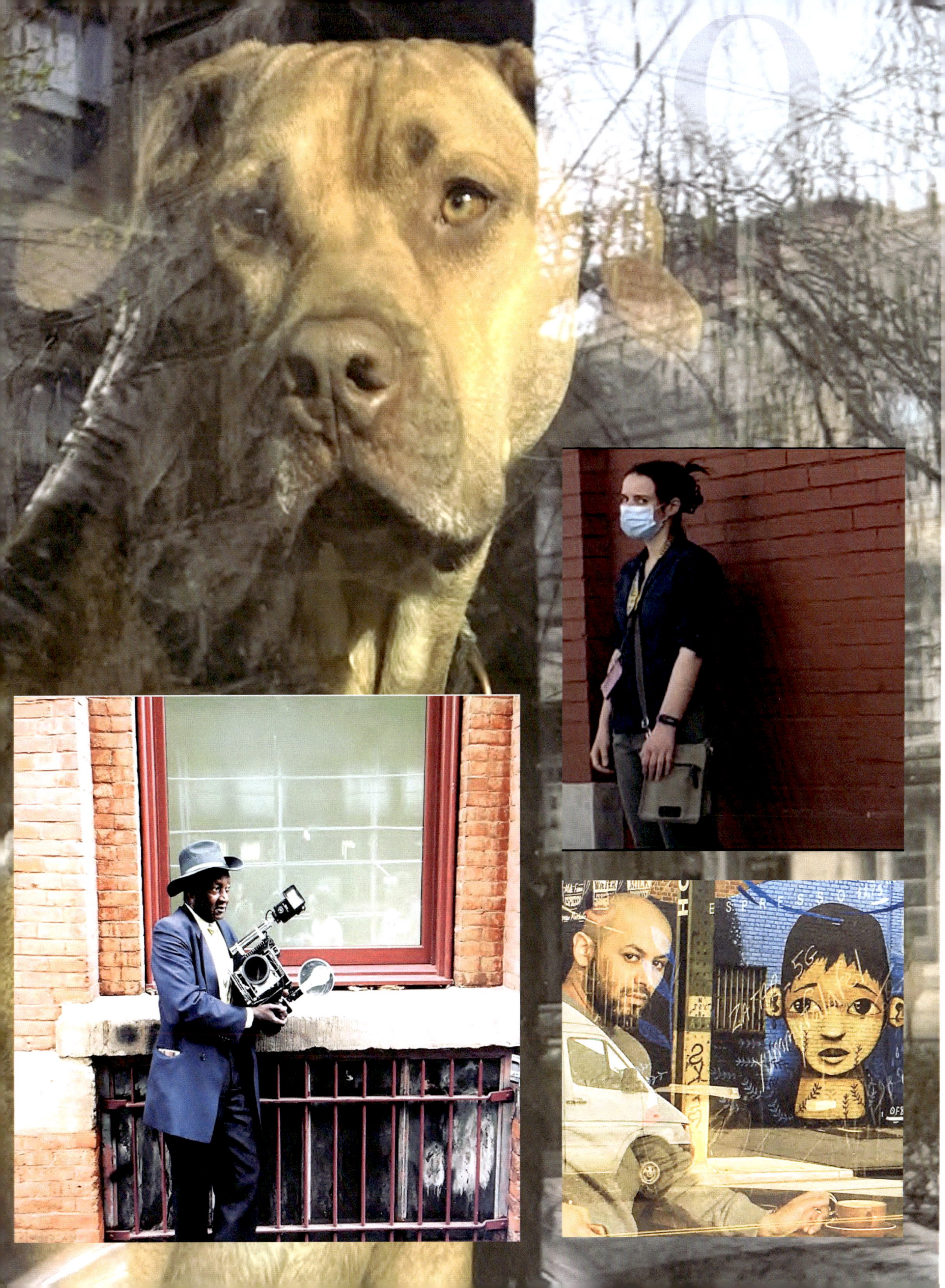

Pare·i·dol·i·a

/ˌperəˈdoleə/

noun

1. the perception of apparently significant patterns or recognizable images,
   especially faces, in random or acci
   dental arrangements of shapes and
   lines:

A RANDOM CONCRETE WALL

Qui·et

/ˈkwiət/

adjective

1. making little or no noise:
2. carried out discreetly, secretly, or with moderation:

noun

1. absence of noise or bustle; silence; calm:

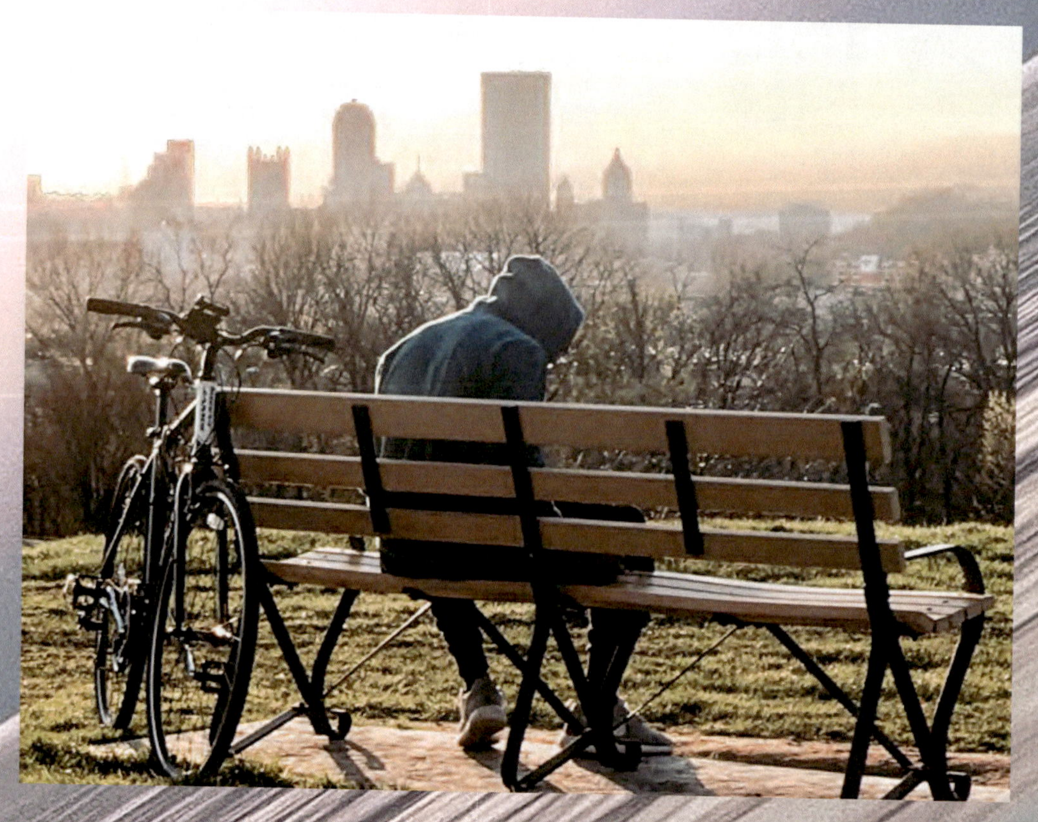

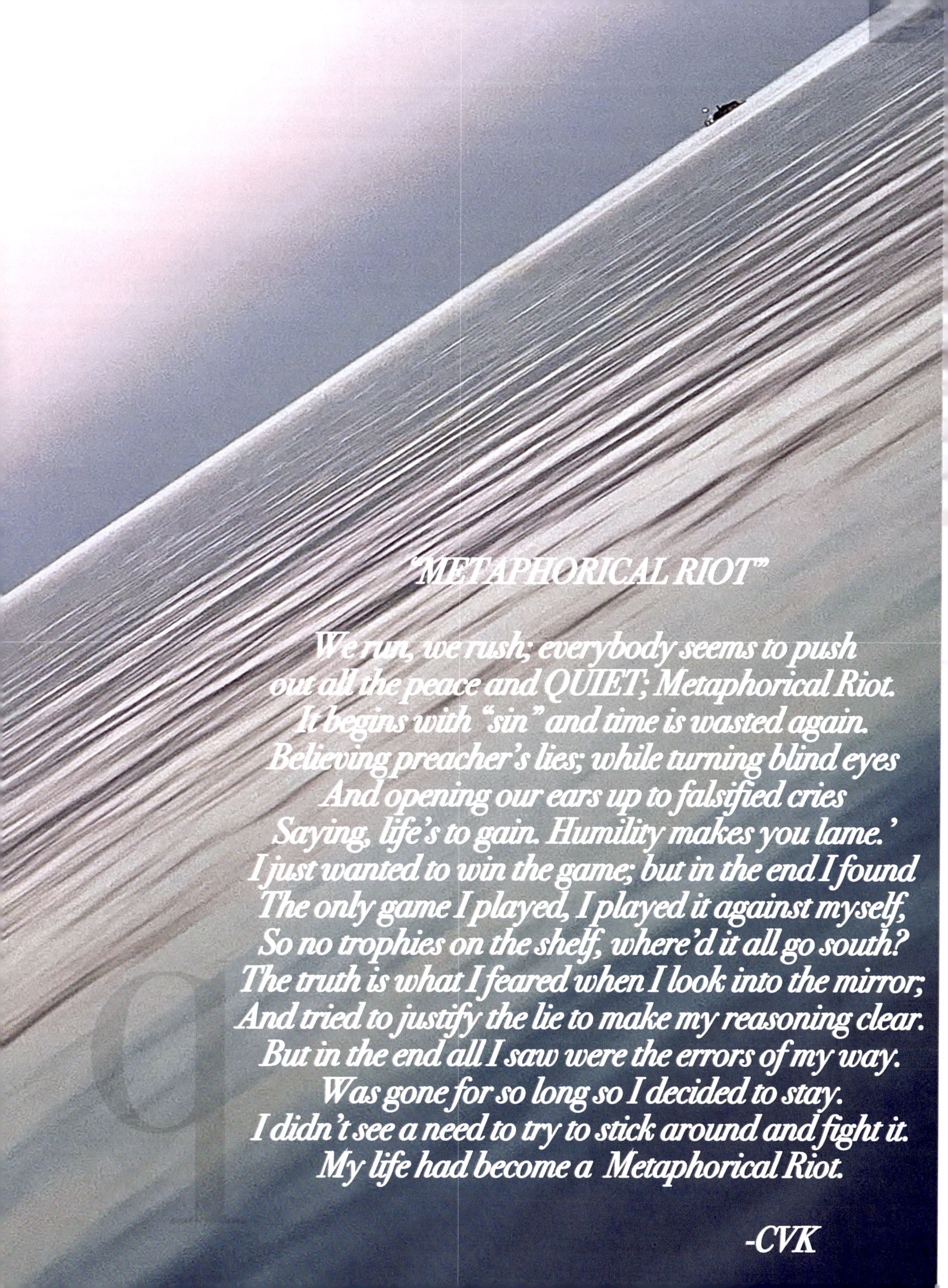

"METAPHORICAL RIOT"

We run, we rush; everybody seems to push
out all the peace and QUIET; Metaphorical Riot.
It begins with "sin" and time is wasted again.
Believing preacher's lies; while turning blind eyes
And opening our ears up to falsified cries
Saying, life's to gain. Humility makes you lame.'
I just wanted to win the game; but in the end I found
The only game I played, I played it against myself,
So no trophies on the shelf, where'd it all go south?
The truth is what I feared when I look into the mirror;
And tried to justify the lie to make my reasoning clear.
But in the end all I saw were the errors of my way.
Was gone for so long so I decided to stay.
I didn't see a need to try to stick around and fight it.
My life had become a Metaphorical Riot.

-CVK

Re·flect

/ree flekt/

verb

1. (of a surface or body) *throw back (heat, light, or sound) without absorbing it.*

2. *think deeply or carefully about:*

"Moscow Mule"

Faithless in the faceless,
made me fall from their graces,
leaving miles of empty spaces
in the vast, empty sea
of false christianity.
The hateful love; by their Bible's deceived.
For who'd have believed
grown men and grown women, scared of a "satan"
they let in their own front doors.
With scores of lures of demands and fear,
from just a boy, 'twas made crystal clear
that life brought sadness; hypocrytical madness,
arrogant fascade, playing children of god,
yet beating their own,
so the second I was grown,
fate helped create my exit,
so now about it I spit,
like the drunk of a "pastor"
as he yelled like a bastard til red in the face,
the name of Christ, disgraced.
For the day after church,
on a barstool he perched,
put liquor on his lips,
as his self-righteousness drips
into a puddle of booze,
where a drunk takes a snooze,
yet more honest a man, than the copper fool,
His REFLECTion, not in Christ,
but a Moscow Mule.

-CVK

Sa·tor·i

/s ə'torē/

noun

1. sudden enlightenment

As summer's forecast turns to chill
The hue of Autumn now paints the hill
No longer green, but golden red,
For Chlorophyll's shine, has briefly fled;
Leaving leaves to leave, a lingering sight;
Their final bow. Supernova's light.
For vibrant leaves, soon fallen 'dead'
Will blanket Earth, then nutrient-fed
by the rustling leaves as they crumble to dust.
This cycle of life, give us pause, it must.
To consider our place in Nature's story
For our planet, our people, need to find SATORI.

-CVK

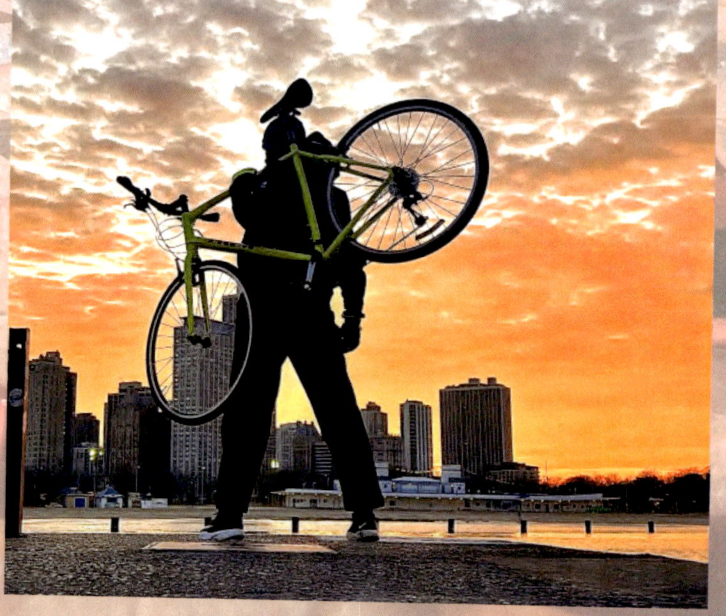

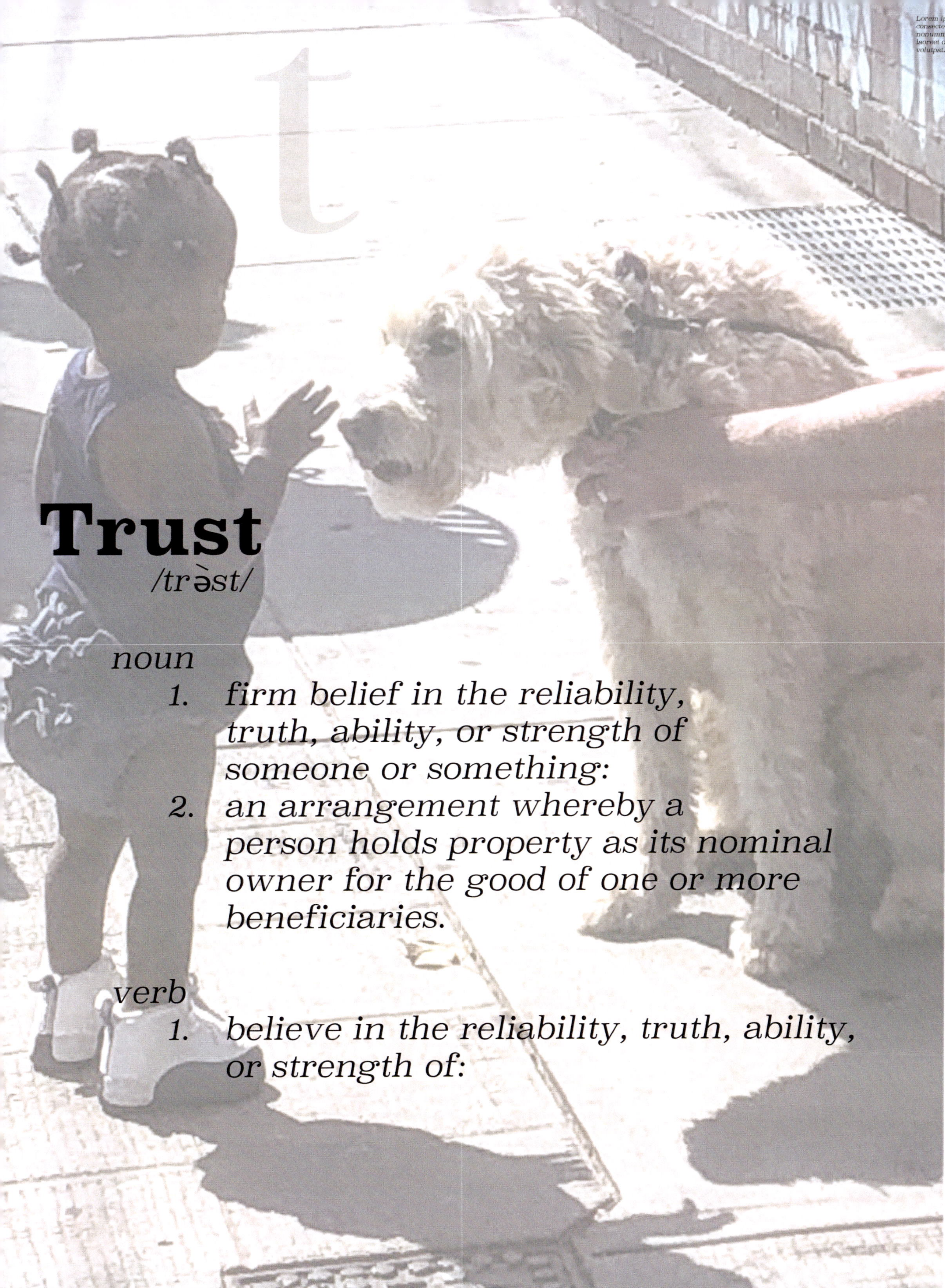

Trust

/trə̀st/

noun

1. firm belief in the reliability, truth, ability, or strength of someone or something:
2. an arrangement whereby a person holds property as its nominal owner for the good of one or more beneficiaries.

verb

1. believe in the reliability, truth, ability, or strength of:

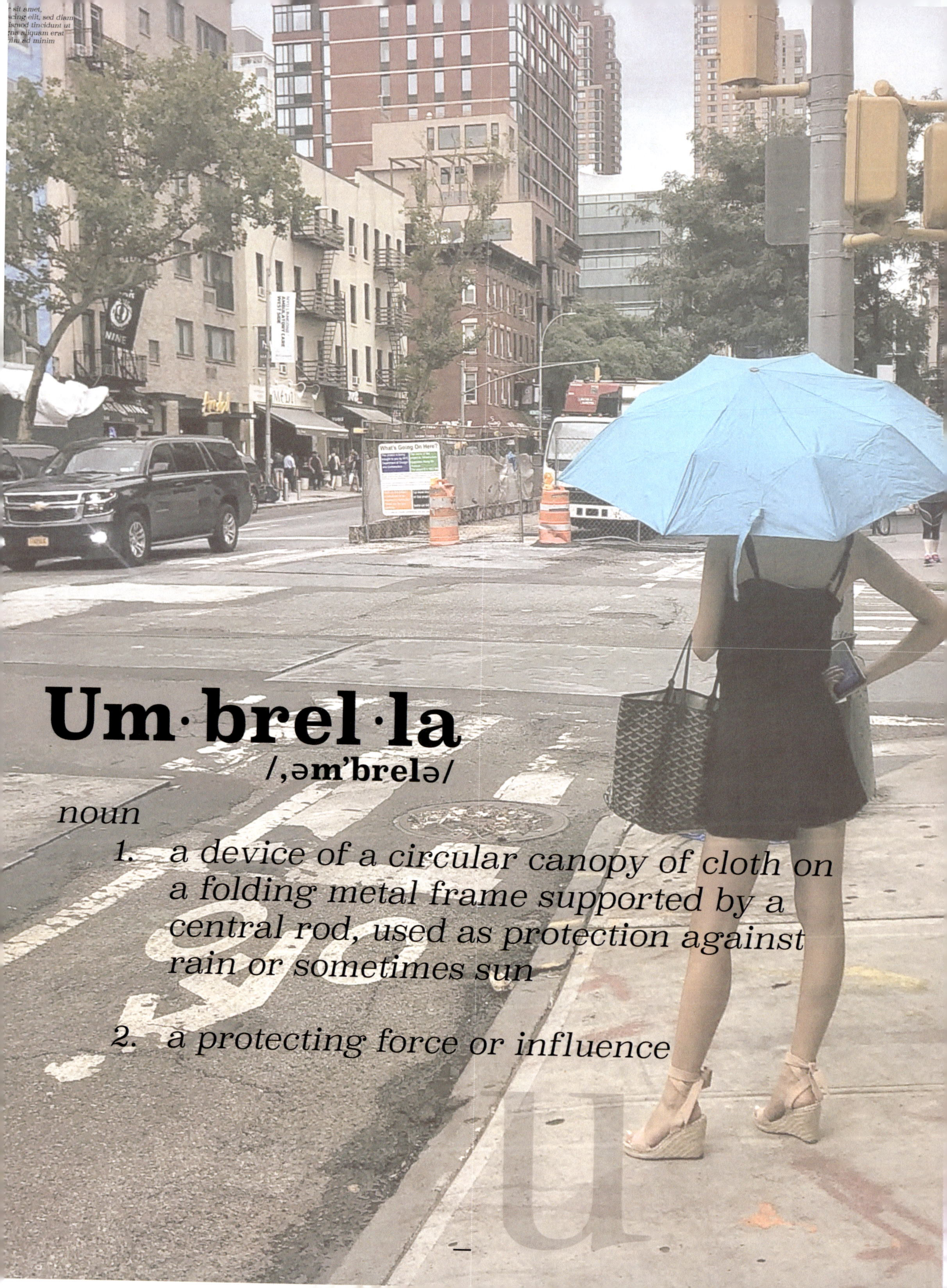

Um·brel·la
/ˌəm'brelə/

noun

1. a device of a circular canopy of cloth on a folding metal frame supported by a central rod, used as protection against rain or sometimes sun

2. a protecting force or influence

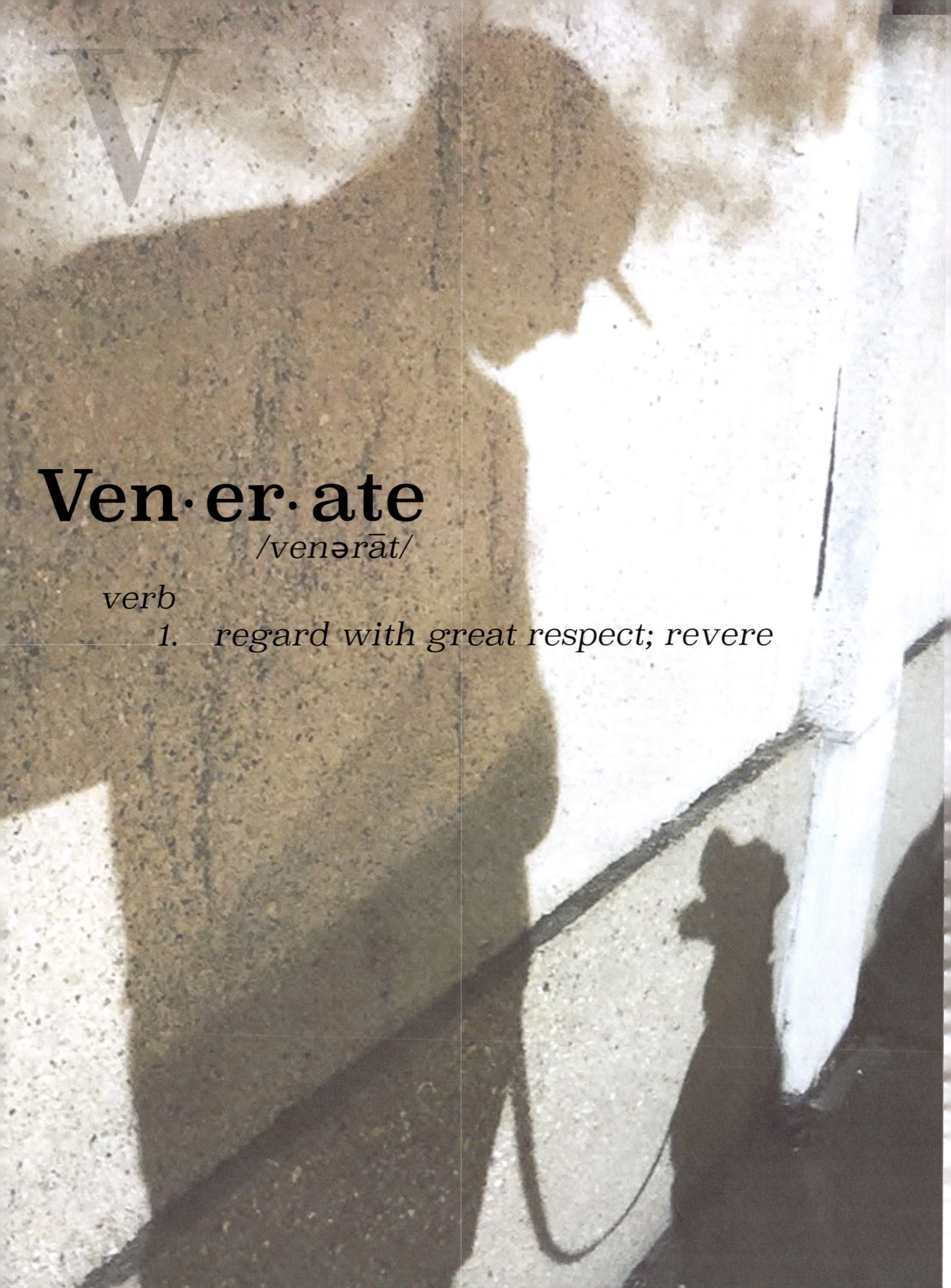

V

Ven·er·ate
/venərāt/

verb
1.   regard with great respect; revere

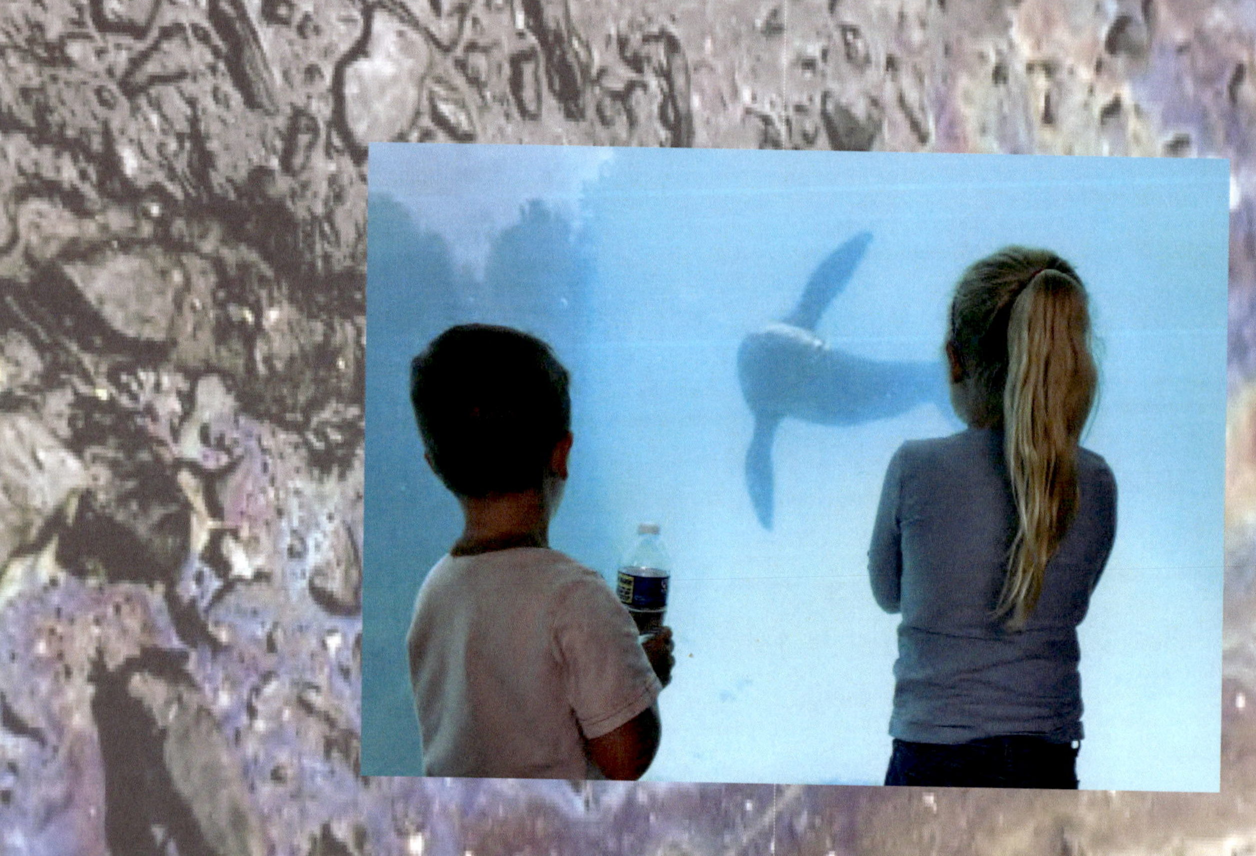

Won·der

/ˈwəndər/

noun

1. a feeling of surprise mingled
    with admiration, caused by
    something beautiful, unexpected.

verb

1. desire or be curious to know
    something
2. feel doubt:

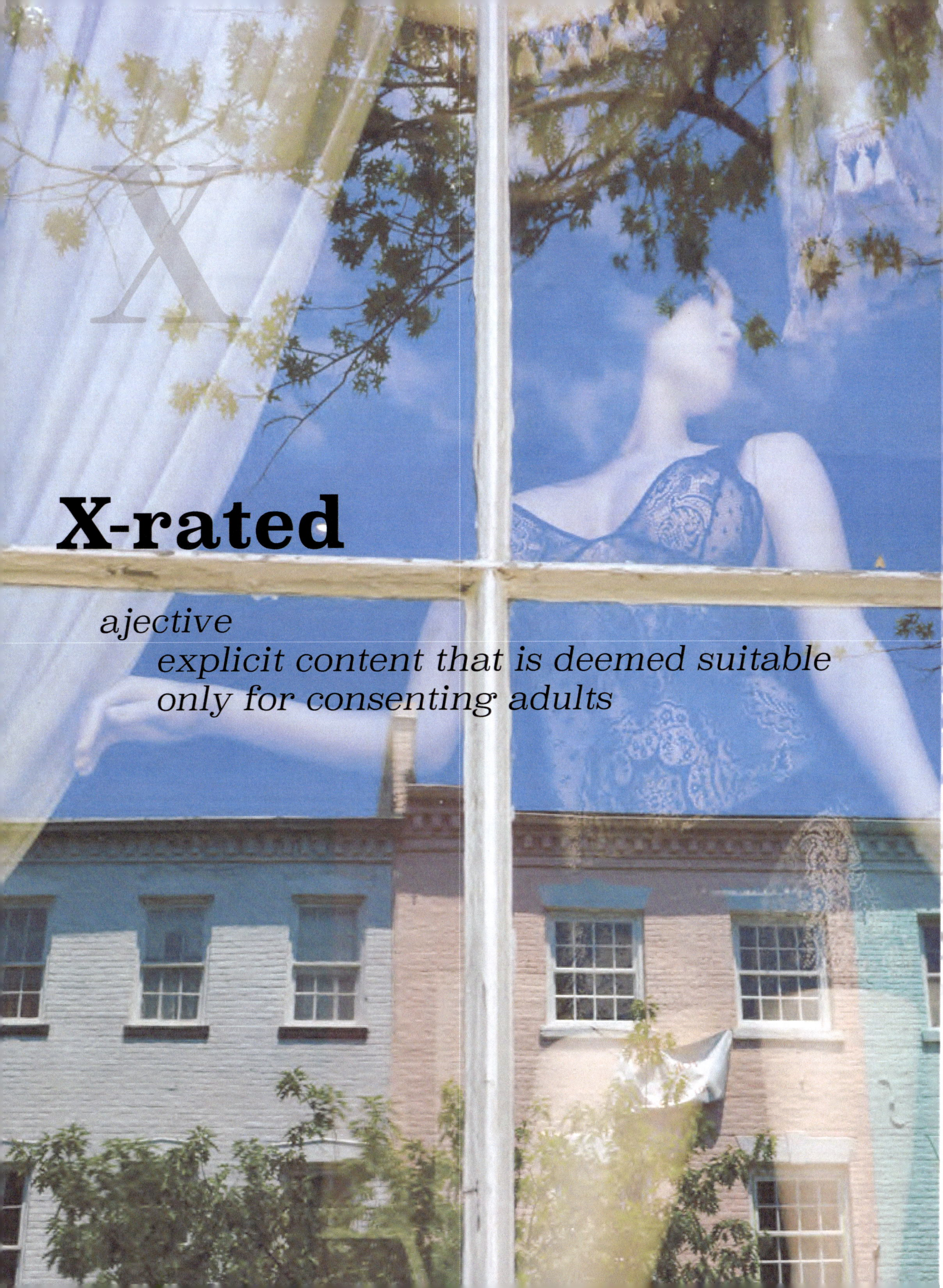

X
X-rated
ajective
    explicit content that is deemed suitable
    only for consenting adults

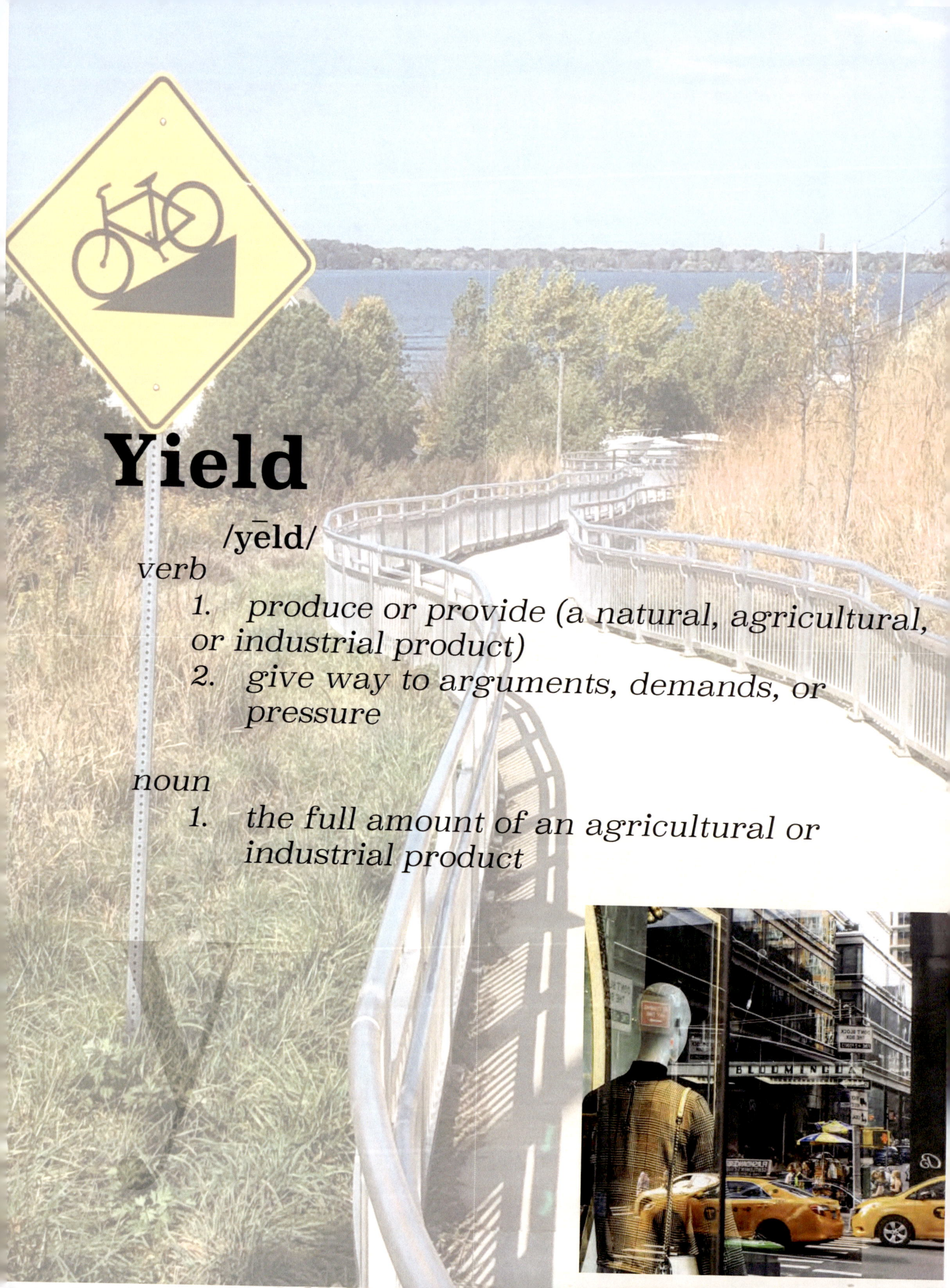

Yield

/yēld/

verb

1.   produce or provide (a natural, agricultural, or industrial product)
2.   give way to arguments, demands, or pressure

noun

1.   the full amount of an agricultural or industrial product

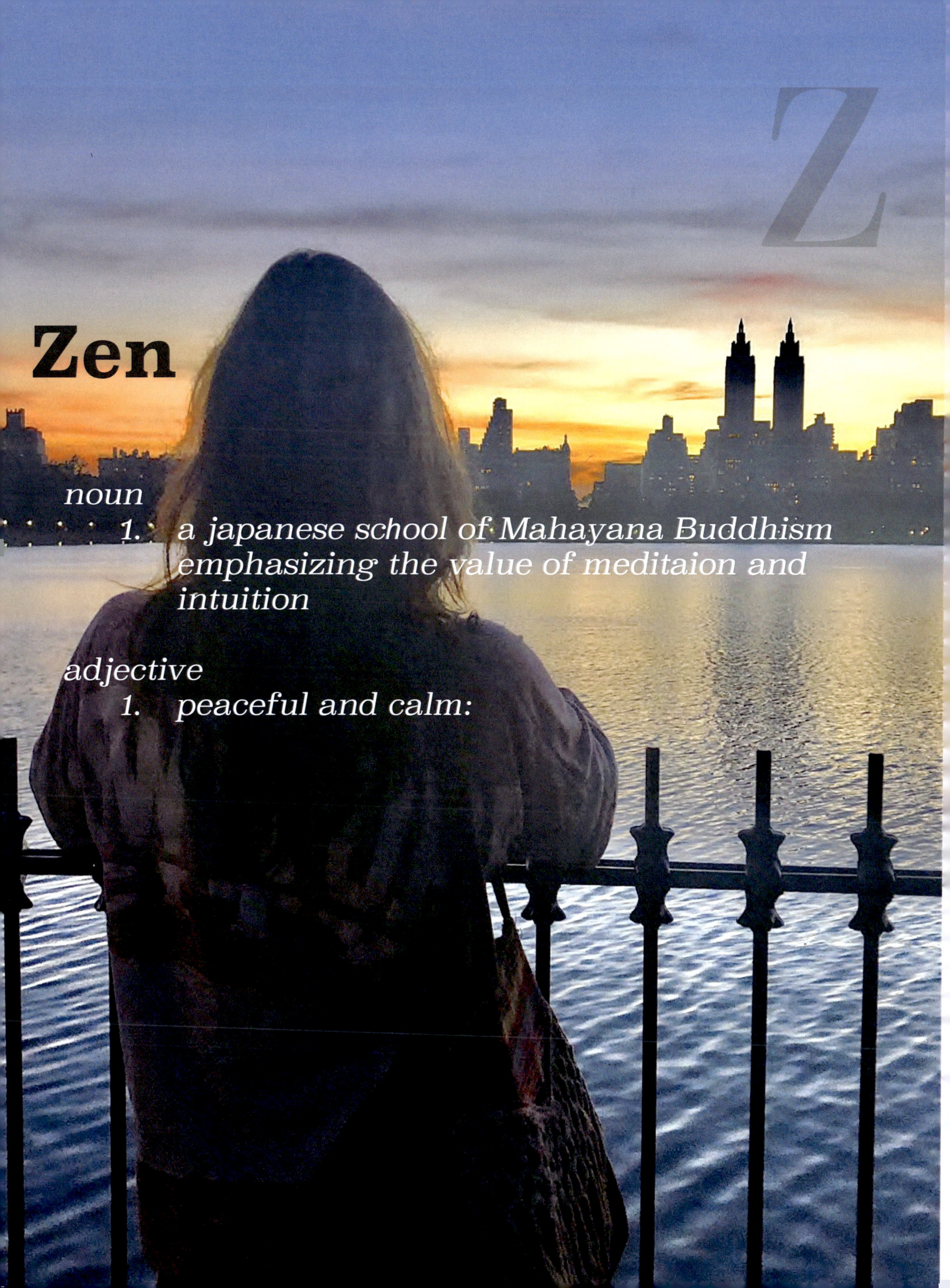

Zen
noun
1. a japanese school of Mahayana Buddhism emphasizing the value of meditaion and intuition

adjective
1. peaceful and calm:

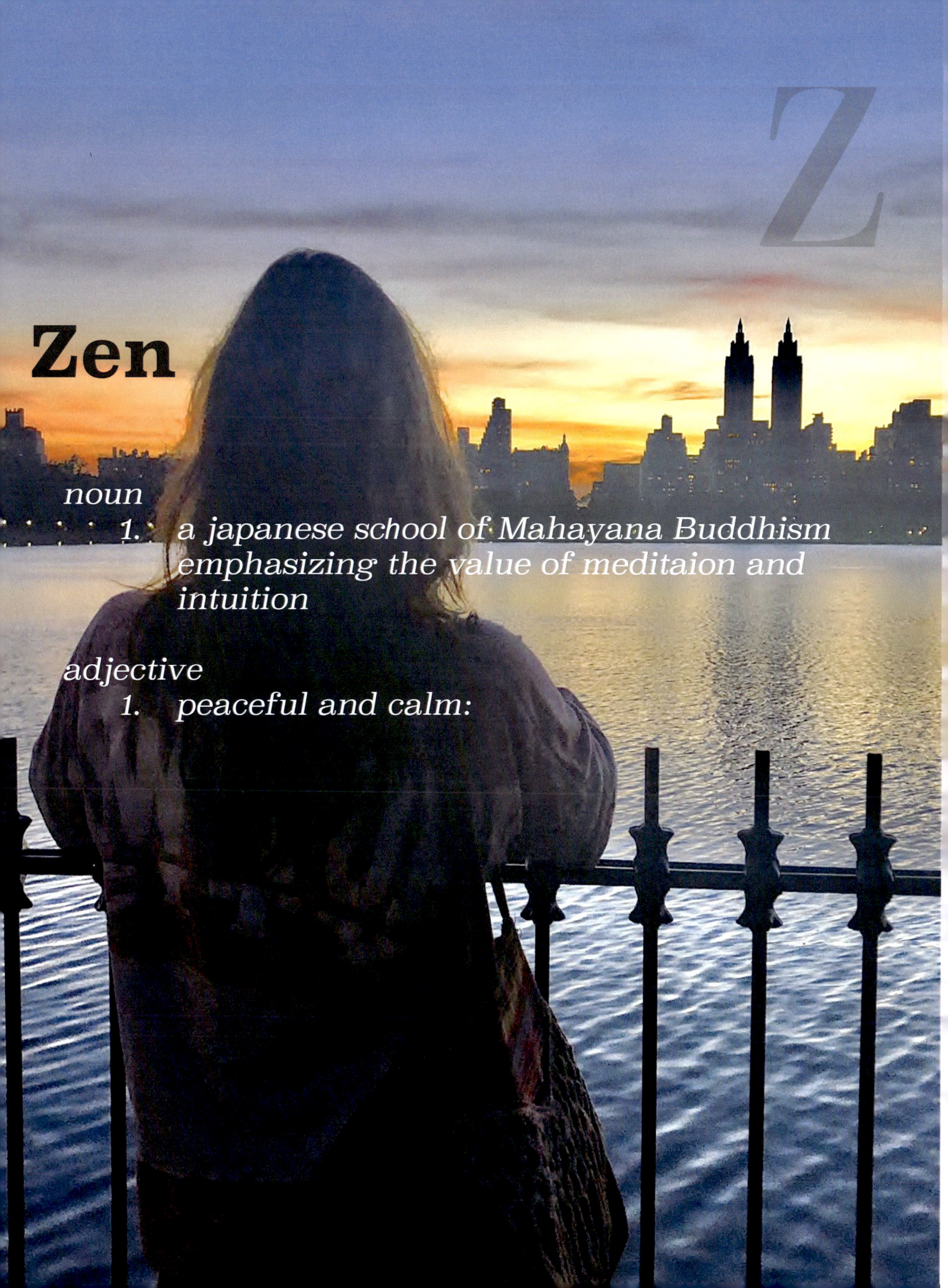
Zen
noun
1. a japanese school of Mahayana Buddhism emphasizing the value of meditaion and intuition

adjective
1. peaceful and calm: